The Power of the Page

Children's Books and their Readers

Pat Pinsent

Published in as_____te

David Fulton Publishers Ltd
2 Barbon Close, London WC1N 3JX

First published in Great Britain by
David Fulton Publishers 1993

Note: The right of the editor to be identified as the editor of this work has been asserted by her in accordance with the Copyright, Designs and Patents Act 1988.

British Library Cataloguing in Publication Data

A catalogue record for this book is available from the British Library

ISBN 1-85346-234-9

Typeset by Textype Typesetters, Cambridge
Printed by Bell and Bain Ltd., Glasgow

Contents

The Roehampton Teaching Studies Series

This new series of books is aimed primarily at student and practising teachers. It covers key issues in current educational debate relating to age phases, school management, the curriculum and teaching methods. Each volume examines the topic critically, bringing out the practical implications for teachers and school organisation.

Authors – not necessarily based at Roehampton – are commissioned by an Editorial Board at The Roehampton Institute, one of the United Kingdom's leading centres of educational research as well as undergraduate and postgraduate training.

The General Editor of the series is Dr Jim Docking, formerly Chairman of the Institute's School of Education.

A selection of recent and forthcoming titles appears on the back cover of this book.

Introduction: Children's Response to Story

'A tale which holdeth children from play and old men from the chimney corner'
(Sir Philip Sidney, c. 1580)

Sue Townsend (*Times Saturday Review*, August 29th 1992) confesses that once she learnt (rather late) to read:

> Reading became a secret obsession: I would drop a book guiltily if anyone came into a room. I went nowhere without a book – the lavatory, a bus journey, walking to school.

Why has story so strong a power of diverting us from what we should be doing, so that we *must* listen or read on, we *must* know what happened next? The almost shame-faced way in which, at a remove of four centuries, Sidney and Townsend talk of their addiction to story probably has echoes in the experience of many readers, and indeed seems to be something fundamental to the whole human race.

Colin Tudge (1989) suggests that the human enthusiasm for narrative arose out of need – to try to work out how other people were likely to behave, and to store information:

> We have evolved as creatures who like telling stories. Unlike computers, we are very bad at facts, but . . . we are very good at attaching meaning to fragments of information, and weaving them, often unconsciously, into a narrative. There is nothing fanciful in this; a story with a logical narrative line is a very economical way of storing information.

This conjecture seems to be supported by what anthropologists have discovered about all cultures, and the importance of story is also fundamental in individual human development. As Meek (1982) points out, 'Children tell their earliest stories as they begin to talk'; narrative is a mode of initiation for them into 'family lore', and 'stories take over the business of sorting out the world'.

Narrative may indeed be vital in the infancy of the race and the individual, but this doesn't in itself imply that it is equally important in later stages of development. However, the academic psychologist and philosopher, Jerome Bruner (1986), makes major claims for the importance of narrative as a mode of cognitive functioning. While admitting the necessity for the kind of thinking encountered in mathematical or scientific thought, which he terms 'paradigmatic', he shows how

> narrative works by contructing simultaneously two landscapes: 'the landscape of action' and . . . 'the landscape of consciousness; what those involved in the action know, think and feel' (Bruner, quoted by H. Rosen in B. Rosen, 1988)

This balance between what happened, and the people who were involved in what happened, is the essence of narrative and while some stories may veer one way or another, the best, the ones we come back to time and time again, live by means of both their plots and their characters.

Bruner's valuation of narrative implies that children, by hearing stories read or told, even before they can read themselves, are learning vital skills without which their cognitive development will be impoverished. This stress on story-telling, oral and written, both to and by children, permeates recent work on the curriculum (see for instance, Howe and Johnson's study of storytelling in the classroom, 1992).

Particularly characteristic of children's enjoyment of a story is the fact that they very often want it retold or reread to them, time and time again. Children rely on adults for this telling and retelling, reading and rereading. Children's literature, particularly for the young child, is in some sense therefore not children's at all. Its writers, its publishers, its booksellers and librarians, its purchasers, and in the early stages, its readers, are adults, and if books are not in some way endorsed by adults the children will not experience them at all.

What then does the adult demand from a book for a child? There are of course certain fairly crude criteria – price, subject matter within the child's grasp, 'suitability' (no sex and violence, for instance). But if the adult is going to admit the child to the full experience of the book, there is a real need for the adult to enjoy it too – time and again and again!

The texts which are discussed in Part One of the present book, 'The Picture and the Story', are ones which can be enjoyed many times, by child and adult – because they have a wealth of different meanings, reinforcing and cutting across each other. Many theorists describe the process of reading texts like these as a transaction, a negotiation of meaning, between text and reader (see Protherough 1983, p.26). The books which appeal most to adults and children have been aptly described by Liz Waterland (in ed. Styles et al., 1992) as 'free range', encouraging the reader to explore the wealth of meaning they offer. She also terms them 'multi-layered' because so many of their meanings need a series of readings in order to be fully appreciated. Some of the meanings of such 'polysemic' texts are only accessible in full with maturity, but some are available to the youngest child more readily than to the adult, who often passes too rapidly over the finer details.

The quality of having many meanings is perhaps particularly character-istic of the marvellous range of picture books now available. In Chapter One of the present volume, Susan Fremantle shows how adults can gain a better understanding of how to read these visual texts, while at the same time the children will be developing not only their language but also their affective response. This latter aspect is pursued further in Sharon Walsh's discussion (Chapter Two) of how polysemic picture books have something to offer children well beyond the age for which they are usually thought suitable; the practical implications of this characteristic are explored in Martin Godleman's account (Chapter Three) of a project involving sec-ondary school pupils with this form of literature. Books with animal char-acters are also a genre of children's literature which attracts a wide range of readers, and some reasons for this width of appeal, within a developmental framework, are explored in Chapter Four.

The antithesis of 'free range' books is 'battery' books, which are pro-duced to order, generally to form part of reading schemes. They tend to have a single level of meaning, strongly associated with a choice of words to reinforce phonic or sight-word skills. Barbara Hearn's research (Chapter Five) into both of these types of books convinced her that the latter lacked the quality of connectedness between words and ideas which is so impor-tant to the enjoyment of the reader of any age. As Waterland (1992) points out, any kind of book, free range or battery, can be used for initial reading teaching; Hearn's work shows that books which have not been written with a controlled vocabulary make as much use of repetition as do 'battery' books. Either sort can be used effectively, but it is unlikely that both will lead to the same kind of attitude to reading – a conjecture supported by a small piece of research (Chieruzzi, 1986) comparing two groups of chil-dren who learnt to read on these contrasting kinds of books. Those who learnt on 'story' books had a much fuller idea of what reading was for and seemed to get much more enjoyment from it.

If Part One of this book focuses particularly on the texts, this does not mean that what the reader brings to the 'negotiation of meaning' can be neglected. Indeed, in looking at animal books, I have found it particularly helpful to use the developmental picture put forward by Appleyard (1990), who, basing his work on both theoretical and empirical studies, suggests a sequence that most readers go through. (This is described in Chapter Four of the present book). A stress on the role of the reader is characteristic of much recent literary criticism, as emphasised in Protherough (1983) and Griffith (1987). Looking at the child reader is, notoriously, made more difficult by children's frequent lack of a vocabulary with which to express their insights. It is clear, however, that given encouragement, children do have some very constructive views about literature. Chapters Six and Seven, in Part Two, report on projects investigating children's responses respectively to fairytales (Susan Fremantle's second piece) and the ever popular series of Enid Blyton (Fiona Collins).

The affective aspect features significantly in several of the chapters in this section. Nicola Humble (Chapter Eight) directs her attention particularly to the way in which books can help children recognise the emotions connected with potentially traumatic experiences, ranging from relationships with step-parents to fear of the dark. In Chapter Eleven, Catherine Sheldon discusses some books which present characters just embarking on adult life and finding the need to define themselves in relation to it. The fantasy framework used in these books makes it easier for the adolescent reader to blend participant and observer roles, identification with and detachment from character.

The practical problem of encouraging children and adolescents to read is tackled in different ways in Chapters Nine and Ten. Children who are competent but unenthusiastic readers may need assistance to develop their own tastes and to know where to look for advice about books, as Philippa Hunt shows, while Jacquie Nunn discusses the implications of a range of research findings which indicate how the attitudes towards reading of upper primary and secondary school children have been affected by both their parents and their teachers.

Part Three focuses on some of the ways in which the outside world impinges on children's literature. As indicated above, adults have a central role in encouraging children to read. But there is often a conflict between what educationalists think children should read, and what popular culture and peer pressure demand. The Cox Report (1989), in its endorsement of literature, quotes the earlier Kingman Report (1988):

> Wide reading, and as great an experience as possible of the best imaginative literature, are essential to the full development of an ear for language. (Section 7.2)

It is clear from what the Report goes on to say (7.5) about the importance of pupils gaining 'a better understanding of the cultural heritage of English literature' that the emphasis is on what might be termed 'good' literature. Yet pupils will often see on television, and bring into the classroom, texts which may be described as 'pulp', or at least ephemeral. Does this matter? Should we virtually exile television from the home and classroom, as Trelease (1984) might appear to wish? It could be argued that television has both inspired many children to read books they would have otherwise found unwelcoming, and given less able readers the chance to join in the dialogue about parts of their 'heritage' which would have otherwise been inaccessible to them. Kim Reynolds (Chapter Twelve) gives some attention to this issue, and also examines what happens to a text which is adapted for television. A related question, explored by Alison Kelly (Chapter Thirteen), is that of the effect on the child reader of the clash in the classroom between their peer culture, subject to media 'hype', and the books which the teacher advocates, the kind of books in fact which are discussed in Part One of the present volume. She shows how an individual pupil resolves this dilemma, and also poses the important question raised by the fact that many 'popular' texts have elements which could be described as objectionable, from an equal opportunities standpoint.

Much of this book inevitably deals with children who do read, or are read to. Story is, however, a marvellous means of bringing into literacy and the book culture those children who have made little progress in learning to read. Mary Walsh (Chapter Fourteen) gives an account of how a policy of using story, both orally and as reading texts, helped a group of less able readers to become enthusiastic about books, and develop their own reading and writing abilities.

None of all the marvellous things which story can do would be possible without the provision of books. Sue Mansfield (Chapter Fifteen) indicates some ways in which teachers and others concerned about children's reading can help children make good use of the wealth of resources available to them in libraries and bookshops.

Narrative is gripping, and the book is the medium which gives the consumer the greatest autonomy, the power to choose the narratives they want to be absorbed in. To appreciate books is a priceless resource. Edward Gibbon (1737–94) describes in his autobiography:

> My early and invincible love of reading, which I would not exchange for the treasures of India.

These words describe what most enthusiastic adult readers feel: the love of reading which we all want children to share.

PART ONE : THE PICTURE AND THE STORY

Chapter One

The Power of the Picture Book

Susan Fremantle

What is your earliest memory of books? Did you have a favourite book, a special person who read to you, or even a place where you hid away to read in private? Have you a memory of a picture which delighted or frightened you, so that you can still feel that unforgettable tingle of excitement or fear?

My most powerful memories are nearly all of pictures: the Christmas tree in *Little Grey Rabbit's Christmas* (Uttley) which appeared fully decorated and blazing with candles on Christmas morning, though who had decorated it the reader never knew. All the magic of Christmas was in that tree and I can feel it now. The terror that gripped me whenever I saw the picture of the Speckledy Hen (in another Uttley book): though I knew the happy ending well, the picture always terrified me to such an extent that my mother glued the pages together to conceal it, thinking to relieve me of my fears. Of course it did no such thing; the Fox lurked even more menacingly between the stuck pages and my fears grew, for if you are helped by a grown-up to run away from something, that surely confirms that it is indeed something truly terrifying.

The circumstances in which a child encounters a book also add to its memorability. The atmosphere and emotions surrounding the child at the time become fused with the images of the story, and thereafter the book arouses feelings not solely engendered by the text.

I have reminisced at some length to give space for your mind to wander, to recall those pictures which were important in your own life, which frightened, delighted, or otherwise impressed you, so that you too can recognise the tremendous power of the visual image.

We live in a highly visual society where the television rather than the book is the major leisure occupation of most children. The moving visual image is an everyday experience, in many ways highly influential. Paradoxically, it is so commonplace that it is frequently ignored. Perhaps worst of all, it is glanced at intermittently, so that it can become a series of unrelated stimuli with no coherence or intelligible story line, sending out confused messages to children who are eating, playing and living out their lives in front of it. In contrast, the unmoving picture book image makes quite different demands on children. Perhaps its greatest advantage is that it is there for revisiting as often as the child wants, so that it can work its magic over and over again. It gives opportunities for ever-deepening encounters, provided the child has the skill to 'read' pictures with the concentration and attention to detail they deserve. Watching television does not necessarily teach such skills.

Indeed, picture books may often be flipped through and then discarded rapidly unless children are taught how to use them. When I give undergraduate students a picture book and watch what they do with it, I nearly always find exactly the same sort of behaviour: a quick flip through, occasional expressions of appreciation, amusement or distaste, and then the book is shut and they sit looking at me with a 'So what? What's next?' expression on their faces. They have to learn how to look at picture books and talk about them as though they were little children. In fact, young children, with fewer preconceptions, are frequently better 'readers' of picture books than adult students. Virginia Lee Burton, author-illustrator (Miller and Field, 1957) recalls the great accuracy of the observations of the world made by her own two small boys: 'Little things interest them, no detail escapes them. (p. 89) Any mistake she made in a picture was spotted by them at once.

Visual Texts

Young children are naturally highly observant and probably rely more on the visual sense than on any other. Their skills with the stable pictorial image as well as with the ubiquitous moving image need, however, to be cherished and reinforced. Teachers may need to relearn these skills, or even to learn them for the first time if they are to help children.

My students are often puzzled by my emphasis on picture book skills, seeing such books as a temporary, pleasurable but babyish stop-gap for the infant or non-reader, not to be lingered over in the process towards 'grown-up books', that is, those with much print and few pictures. When children can read one of these, they are 'there', they are reading 'properly', and teachers can breathe a sigh of relief and turn to other things.

Such a view ignores the riches picture books have to give to the child.

They are not only vital in the teaching of reading, which includes understanding what a book really is and learning how to deal with its demands on the reader (see Meek, 1988). They are also an end in themselves, often of far greater value to the readers and their personal growth and development than many of the all-print books that are written for the younger age-group. These latter have to take into account the young age of the 'listener', for they are usually read aloud and incidentally thus available only to those who can claim the attention of an adult with time to read to them. The language, both vocabulary and syntax, of such books needs to be relatively simple, and they are usually quite short. This means a straightforward plot with very limited description of people, places and feelings, not linguistically very interesting. Humour (which for the youngest relies so much on visual image) is much harder to portray through words alone. This is a pity, for humour is one of the most widely loved and demanded features of all children's books, as many surveys of children's reading (listed for instance in Pain-Lewins and Kinnell, 1989) reveal. It is a way into books for many children.

The story in the best picture books is contained at least as much in the pictures as in the words. When there is real integration of images and the message, the two form an indivisible whole; there is a harmony which strengthens the impact of the book upon the reader. Meaning is absorbed from the whole experience, and unknown language and unfamiliar syntax do not become insurmountable obstacles to understanding. For example, when 'Max made mischief of one kind and another' (in Sendak, *The Wild Things*), the context, the language and the pictures leave the reader in no doubt as to what is meant by 'mischief' and 'of one kind and another'. A word and a structure which were unfamiliar before may now become absorbed into children's understood language, if not yet into their own 'performance' language.

With picture books in which illustrations merely support or decorate parts of the text but do not carry the essential message, children may still have much enjoyment. But they must rely more heavily on the verbal text which may not be fully understood. In this case there is little they can do to help themselves. Their engagement with the text could well be diminished by this reduction in pictorial clues, leaving them less emotionally involved and more like passive by-standers than active meaning makers. It is this active involvement of children with text that is the objective of teachers, both in the early picture book stage and in all later stages of reading. It is not something which simply 'happens' later; early training is essential and picture books are the ideal medium.

At a more practical level, it is also important that children have, as early as possible, the experience of 'reading' a book (by the visual clues) and behaving like readers. They may read to themselves, their toys or a friend; they gain great pleasure and the enhanced self-esteem their 'reading' brings. They can return frequently to the book on their own, without having to depend on a busy adult, enjoying themselves, understanding increasingly more of its message and gaining the benefits of practice.

Picture Books and Growth

At a deeper level, children have a chance to make new meanings on each repeated reading, determined by their own increasing experience of life and of books, and their own personal growth in understanding and feeling. Books, especially picture books, give the space to experience a sustained emotion, to ponder at leisure and to make journeys back and forth into the text.

Much depends, therefore, on the teacher's ability to choose picture books which work at different levels and which are worth repeated encounters. From such books, children gain fresh insights about the world and themselves, and they bring these insights to a fresh reading of the book. Really great books not only help children to grow, they grow with the children.

What do children themselves demand of a picture book? They have no inkling of the power of books in their personal growth. All that is relevant to them is pleasure. Above all, a book is for enjoyment and if the match between book and child fails, all else fails. Young children are egocentric, their world and concerns are paramount. But that does not entail an endless succession of rather banal stories based on visits to the supermarket, lost toys or cleaning teeth. Children are also curious and love to pretend, for how else can they find out who they are except by 'trying-on' other characters and situations? Children certainly need to be able to relate to the books they choose, but that does not entail exact mirror images of themselves and their world. A book need only provide just sufficient links for the child to relate to it, and such links can be subtle indeed. Max (in *The Wild Things*, by Sendak) does not look like any ordinary human girl or boy; some might think he looks more like a sort of fairy tale character. Yet all children (regardless of gender and colour) can relate to his naughtiness and punishment, his adventures and finally his desire to return home to 'where someone loves him best of all'.

In today's multicultural classroom, we rightly emphasise the need to value the background of each child, and so we try to include the literature of many cultures, and pictures including children of different races. Similarly we include a variety of books in which girls and women play active roles. Lavender (in Grugeon and Walden, 1978) points out that it is not necessarily the material environment of a story that is important to a child. It is the 'recognizability of the experience', and the deeper level of identification the child can make with feeling or situation that is more important than superficial resemblances such as eating fish and chips or living in a detached house or a flat. Any child, whatever their colour or gender, can relate to Max's feelings, and similarly any child can relate to Sean in *My Brother Sean* (Breinburg, 1973) crying on his first day at school. Cushla certainly related to him when she kissed his howling picture face to cheer him up (Butler, 1979), despite the difference of race.

Young children themselves generally expect a picture to tell a story. Author-illustrator Marc Simont (Kingman, 1965, p. 178) recalls the many children he has watched drawing. They are aiming to tell an exciting story rather than to create a beautiful picture. They mutter, as they draw, about the actions of their creations:' . . . and the lion comes running down the street . . . and the Indians are hiding behind the rocks, and . . .'

To children, story is all-important; they create it themselves when they tell us about their own lives and they expect it from us and their books. However we should remember that what interests children is often not at all what adults expect. (Lee Burton, in Miller and Field, 1957). Another author-illustrator, Duvoisin (Miller and Field, 1957) points out that children have neither good nor bad taste in illustration; taste is something which is of no concern to them. He makes a very important point:

> What they like is an illustration that suggests something which their imagination can grasp and build upon. (p. 170)

The appeal of books to children's imagination is again emphasised by Sweeney (1957). He links the power of the picture book, its appeal to the child's imagination, and the active nature of the reader's response:

> A child's book is essentially a work of visual art-something that speaks directly to the eye and through the eye. It is a source of education to be sure, but never merely a vessel for the conveyance of information . . . It should be aimed primarily to stimulate the imagination through the eye – to educate in the true sense, *by drawing something out of the observer* [my italics] – to mature the observer through stimulation, to exercise the imagination and develop the power for creating images.
>
> (in Miller and Field, 1957, p. 313)

The observer's role is a highly active one. A book does not work its magic simply by existing, by being looked at casually with minimal effort from the reader. Readers must engage with the text both emotionally and cognitively. Only then will it give them images to think with, 'to organise . . . experiences . . . into a conception of the world' (Meek, 1977, p. 5).

Mediating Between Children and Picture Books

To those who ask how children can be helped to this engagement with text, the answer is twofold: by appropriate *choice of books* and by *talk*. As teachers with a vast amount of great potential material at our disposal, we must understand something of the child's development, be acquainted with a wide range of picture books, and ultimately be prepared to exercise our own judgement. The findings of surveys and research regarding children's tastes and preferences are generally inconclusive. To research such a subject is difficult, and our own observations and memories may well be as good a guide as any.

Talk is the obvious link between the child and the book. It is the means whereby children make their encounter with the book an active one. They become 'makers of meaning', relating the text to their own lives and gaining new perspectives of the world. They grow emotionally and in their own understanding. Inevitably they grow in language as well, by absorbing it from books, but most of all, from using it in discussion.

Children's experiences of picture books are likely to be different according to whether they are reading with adults, other children, or alone. In solitude, a child communes with a book, drawing upon past experiences of life and other books. The links are made purely by thought or by 'inner speech', occasionally uttered aloud as a sort of monologue. The value here is largely to do with the message. In the best picture books, story line, atmosphere, emotions, even causal connections are all depicted in the colour, style and details of the pictures, as in *Rosie's Walk* (Hughes, 1969), *The Wild Things* (Sendak, 1967) or *The Wild Washerwoman* (Yeoman, 1962). The observant child receives much food for thought and personal growth, as well as great enjoyment. The more multilayered and skilfully created the book, the greater the potential for the child's response, and the greater the likelihood of frequent returns to ponder it again. Young children lack the knowledge to grasp the subtleties of emotion and atmosphere from language alone but from pictures they can take as much as their capabilities and development allow. And in many picture books, there's more for next time too.

In a pair or group, children similarly draw upon their past experiences and talk together about themselves and the book. Few people today would doubt the value of the talk of young children, not least for its social interaction. Language skills are involved in the sharing of enthusiasm, of bits which are puzzling, and of connections between themselves and the book. They can gossip, drawing upon their lives and memories of other books. Chambers (1983) calls this 'talk about the book and me' (p. 164).

If an adult is involved, similar talk can emerge, and the opportunities for teacher and children together are even greater. Wells (1986) underlines the value of such discussion about a story:

> Such an experience is not only an introduction to literacy but also an entry into a shared world that can be explored through the sort of collaborative task that is the most effective way of facilitating children's learning and language development. (pp.159/160)

The teacher or other adult can encourage the children to venture into new areas of understanding, to deepen their response, to grasp at things only dimly perceived, to talk about the meaning of the book itself. (cf. Chambers, 1983) The opportunities for personal growth are great, and those for language development are perhaps even greater.

It might be argued that I have overstated the case for the importance of discussion about picture books. The evidence, however, is extensive: White (1954) with Carol, Butler (1979) with Cushla, and the Cragos (1983) with Anna, all provide fascinating evidence of children learning about books, about life, and about themselves, and also of acquiring the language to talk about it all.

But, above all, what must *not* happen is for such a child/adult discussion to turn into a question-and-answer session, with the adult knowing all the answers! This will curb the children's responses and their language too. For real response, *all* participants must be equal and genuinely sharing the pleasures and emotions of the book, and helping each other to articulate those half-perceived ideas at the fringes of awareness. When no-one's opinion is of more value than anyone else's, children will not only increase their response and develop their language, but their self-esteem and motivation will be enhanced as well.

It is incidentally interesting to read of a study in which nursery children were tested for language skills both before and after a four month period of work with picture books. A control group had no such picture book experiences. While both groups scored more highly after four months, presumably partly because of environmental and developmental factors, the scores of the experimental group were sufficiently ahead of those of the control group for the researchers to conclude the that supplementary instruction with picture books had had a positive effect on the children's language (Ari and Gonen, 1989). While recognising the limitations in this project, both of the rather formal nature of the tests (Peabody Picture Word Vocabulary Test and the Language Developmental Levels of the Stanford Binet Intelligence Scale) and of the process of testing children as young as these, it is nevertheless some tangible objective evidence of language development through picture books. Most teachers would feel subjectively that work with picture books is very valuable; they cannot always prove it to the satisfaction of parents and those in authority.

Finally, to the skills of 'reading' a picture book, skills which are useful not only to teachers and young children but to older children too. There are many excellent picture books for children of nine to thirteen (Moss, 1981), whose content will stretch their emotions and understanding as powerfully as any other book. Much valuable picture book literature will, however, be closed to children who have not been taught such skills early in life.

Teachers need to become skilled themselves in 'reading' picture books before they can pass it on; my undergraduates demonstrate the need for this learning to occur. This requires *time* – not necessarily a lot, but enough to change our 'reading' of picture-books from a quick flip through to active contemplation. It is often a matter of appreciating the importance of the genre and of changing our own habits. If at the end of every book we assume that something has been missed and there is more richness in it, we have made a good start.

It also helps to read writers who are more skilled than ourselves in this process; authors I have found particularly helpful are Heeks (1981), Knundsen Linauer (1988), Wright (1984) and Tucker (1971 and 1981). To work one's way through a book in detail, following step-by-step the ideas and perceptions of others (even if we do not agree with all of them) gives valuable practice. For example, Jane Doonan, in 'Talking Pictures: A New Look at *Hansel and Gretel*' (1983) takes the reader through Anthony Browne's version of the fairy tale, teaching us how to observe and to make deductions from the smallest detail. Ultimately, however, there is no substitute for our own ideas for there are no right answers which another person can teach us.

Work through books slowly with a friend, or in a teachers' workshop, and enjoy them freely *at your own level*, not trying to look at them from a child's perspective (that can come later). If we cannot relate to books and enjoy them ourselves in our own way, why are we trying to teach children how to do it?

Lastly, enjoy them with children. Let *them* teach *you*. Just for once we need not know any answers. If we have succeeded in choosing books which all can relate to, providing something for everyone whatever their background, tastes or culture, we will ensure many hours of satisfying reading. All the children need is 'space' and freedom from our expectations. Perhaps that's what we need too.

Books referred to in this chapter

Breinberg, P. (1973) *My Brother Sean*. London: Bodley Head
Browne, A. (1981) *Hansel and Gretel*. London: Julia MacRae
Hutchins, P. (1969) *Rosie's Walk*. London: Bodley Head
Sendak, M. (1967) *Where the Wild Things Are* London: Bodley Head
Uttley, A. (1940) *Little Grey Rabbit's Christmas* London: Collins

14

Uttley, A. (1945) *The Speckledy Hen*. London: Collins
Yeoman, J. (1962) *The Wild Washerwomen*. Harmondsworth: Penguin

Chapter Two

The Multi-layered Picture Book

Sharon Walsh

Literacy today cannot be restricted to the printed word. The culture of the western world surrounds children with a myriad of signs and symbols from the moment they are born. Much everyday communication is in graphic form, or may be in a combination of written text, symbol and picture. The images provided by the television screen, street sign advertising, newspapers, junk mail and books are an integral part of contemporary life.

The combining of picture and written text to make a narrative whole is a commonplace formula used by the producers of glossy magazines and the designers of roadside billboards alike. In its dual symbolic representations of visual image and text, the picture book offers the reader a micro reflection of contemporary literacy. It draws on many of the conventions of the modern media. Like television, it uses freeze frame, close up, image overlaid with text and flashback. Unlike the fleeting images of television however, the sequence of still pictures and text in the picture book allows for each individual reader's variations in pace.

The picture book genre has traditionally been regarded as one to be used by young readers who are still in need of picture cues to support the decoding of the written text. Picture books produced with this in mind generally offer the reader a simplistic written text, which is reflected in the accompanying illustrations. But to view the whole picture book genre simply as a tool for use in the beginning stages of reading is to underestimate its worth.

The multi-layered picture book contains brief written texts and accompanying pictures, but such is the complexity in the seemingly simple format that these books offer challenges to both the adult and young reader. Picture and written text are interrelated to contain more than one definitive narrative.

Personal experience and expectations are drawn on as the reader moves towards an interpretation of the book. The reader must actively select from the many symbolic representations of meaning in both the pictures and the written text, so making decisions about the direction of the narrative.

Wolfgang Iser (1978) describes the active reader as a co-author. The text alone is simply an inanimate object, a collection of marks on the page which serve to offer the reader a narrative framework. The creative imagination of the reader is relied on to fill the gaps in the framework and so complete the work of the writer. The response to the marks is as individual as the reader. Each completion of the narrative is created in the active interaction between the individual reader and the unique text.

Young readers need to be encouraged to take an active role in the reading of the multi-layered picture book. The adult reader must model a questioning approach to these texts, in which the reading of the picture is seen to be as important as the reading of the written text. The pictures need to be initially scanned and then unpicked, for each page demands careful attention. Such readings cannot be hurried and indeed many texts need to be revisited on several occasions, revealing new layers of meaning on each reading.

In its ability to deal with complex issues in an apparently simple format, the multi-layered picture book draws its readership from all members of the literacy club, a term used by Frank Smith (e.g. 1988, p.1). The sharing of these texts can be as challenging to the adult reader as to the child. The unpicking of the different layers, and subsequent piecing together of the narrative, is wholly dependent on the experience that the individual reader brings to the task. The adult reader will inevitably fill the gaps in the narrative framework in a different way to the inexperienced reader. In any single sharing of the text, adult and child may realise a different global narrative.

The contemporary picture book genre explores all aspects of the human condition. The reader shares the personal relationships, fears, hopes, failings and triumphs of the characters in the book. In doing so, some readers must confront and reassess aspects of their own lives.

Such texts 'reveal what we think we have successfully concealed even from ourselves.' (Meek, 1988, p. 35). The picture extends the meaning begun in the written text so that even the young child is offered the opportunity to develop complex emotional and cognitive understandings, normally inaccessible to the inexperienced reader.

Parent and child together can reflect on their abilities to communicate to each other as they read David McKee's *Not Now Bernard*. The brief text does not acknowledge Bernard's loneliness and ignores his transformation into a monster. So too do his preoccupied parents. The reader must actively turn to the pictures to fill the gaps in the written narrative and, in doing so, explore personal fears of rejection and loneliness. In its few pages of brief text and accompanying pictures, this simple book also manages to challenge parent readers to reassess the quality of their parenting.

In the picture book *In the Attic* (Oram and Kitamura) the reader must accompany a boy in an exploration of the world in his attic. The author has provided a minimal text which contrasts with the highly coloured but ambiguous pictures to activate the imagination of the reader. The reader must piece together a personal reading of the narrative from the written and picture text. Like the boy featured in the book, the reader can create a new narrative on each return to the attic. The adult reader, unlike the boy's Mother, must be ready to suspend disbelief and, temporarily at least, open the window of imagination in order to create the narrative.

One prolific author-illustrator has made an outstanding contribution to the genre of the multi-layered picture book. The distinctive texts of Anthony Browne challenge the reader at different levels, employing images of humour and pathos in quickly changing patterns which not only hold the attention to the end but often demand a re-reading.

> '. . . . what's the use of a book,' thought Alice, 'without any pictures or conversations?' (from *Alice's Adventures in Wonderland* by Lewis Carroll, illustrated by Anthony Browne, 1988).

Browne engages in conversation with his readers in his written and visual texts. Writer and reader must each contribute to the conversation, the one providing the multi-layered framework, the other bringing personal experience to the unpicking of the symbolic representations. The co-authors can then reflect on many issues relevant to contemporary society, as well as those of a more personal nature. Browne's texts explore social relationships within the domestic setting, celebrating the achievements of ordinary people without pronouncing judgements on their failings.

When the Smiths and the Smythes take their dogs for *A Walk in the Park*, the reader shares in the delight of two children's friendship, which contrasts markedly with their class-divided parents' inability to communicate. The young reader can respond to the visual jokes which the author has scattered throughout the text, but must then puzzle over their contribution to the narrative. The adult reader can enjoy the somewhat humorous references to class in the stereotypical names of the characters, and then reflect on their impact on the global narrative. In both cases, the readers must bring previous experiences to the reading of the symbolic representations of meaning in the visual and written text.

In *Willy the Wimp* and *Willy the Champ* Browne invites the reader to laugh at the gentle Willy's misguided attempts to be macho, but this layer of the narrative is underpinned by the more serious suggestion that real heroes are made from within. As Willy and his friend Millie go for a walk they pass by an identical backdrop to that in *A Walk in the Park* in which the original characters have been humorously transformed into apes.

The gorilla-like figure is a recurring theme in Browne's texts. It joins other distinctive leitmotifs such as Fair Isle sweaters, rainbows, walls, and anthropomorphic tree trunks as well as several images borrowed from the work of the surrealist painter René Magritte. All of the symbols provide cross references in Browne's multi-layered texts so that the reader must become a member of the Anthony Browne Club in order to fully respond to the images in each text.

Frank Smith suggests (1983, p. 17) that, 'without metaphor thought is inert, and with the wrong metaphor, it is hobbled.' Browne's metaphors are presented in both written and pictorial form. To refer to the latter as 'illustrations' would be to imply that they serve merely to clarify the text. Browne's pictures, however, bridge the gaps which the written narrative is unable to fill with words.

In *Gorilla*, Hannah lives alone with her busy Father. In one picture, Hannah waits to ask her Father a question. The reader stands behind Hannah as she hesitatingly waits, feet together, hands behind her back, for her Father to look up from his desk. Hannah's anxiety and subsequent disappointment are written in the pictures, not in the written text.

Browne's text and pictures combine to make a unified whole but they do not necessarily complete the narrative. The individual reader must make a series of decisions in the reading of his texts. In *Piggybook*, the reader must carefully scrutinize the detailed pictures and must decide whether to take up Browne's challenge of examining an exposé of stereotypical gender roles, or simply to enjoy the book for its humour. In *Bear Goes To Town* the bear literally draws the reader into the narrative. Such are the layers in this picture book that the reader can read a simple tale of animal adventure, an allegory on the lives of farm animals destined for slaughter or a more sinister metaphor of Nazi persecution.

A family of four spend one day together in the *Zoo*. More concerned with their squabbles and with eating, the father and two boys show no empathy for the plight of the caged animals. In contrast, the mother gazes in silence into each enclosure and cage. The reader can observe the behaviour of both the family and the animals in turn. The written text extends the story of the family as presented in the pictures, but there are no words to accompany the pictures of the animals. Browne leaves his readers with the question 'Do you think animals have dreams?' In responding to this the reader must reread the text and so become a co-author in the creation of each of the animal's personal narrative.

In *The Visitors Who Came to Stay* Browne's pictures interweave with a text by Annalena McAfee to offer a glimpse into the life of Katy and her single parent father who live alone by the sea and 'she liked it that way'. Her routine lifestyle is interrupted by the visit of her father's new girlfriend Mary and her son Sean. They become regular visitors, and eventually come to stay. Their intrusion into Katy's life is made worse by Sean's endless supply of practical jokes which, far from amusing, serve only to irritate Katy.

McAfee's simple text contrasts with Browne's detailed pictures which are in turn both humorous and bizarre. Initially the picture and written text balance each other, but it is largely through the pictures that the reader begins to witness the disintegration of the harmony in Katy's life.

When Katy and the reader are first introduced to the visitors they are already inside her home. They stand in the brightly lit hallway, ready to step into a living room. Katy stands facing the visitors and her anxiety is reflected on the facial expression of her tightly held teddy bear. The picture is dominated by a large bookcase, which is sectioned to contain several of Magritte's surrealistic images. In addition, the room contains a chair which hovers above the ground. The reader must relate these puzzling images to the realistic context in which they are placed. Illusion and reality have become fused in a way that is both humorous and disturbing. The composite picture offers a parallel reading of Katy's psyche and her outer world.

Browne offers both his reader and Katy chances and choices. Katy can be the victim of Sean's jokes, or she can enjoy her new found friendship. She can mourn the loss of her father's undivided attention or she can celebrate the formation of a new family. In the final full-plate Katy and her father stand outside the gate of Mary and Sean's house. Through its likeness to a fruit machine, the house appears to offer Katy and her father the chance of a new life whilst acknowledging the risk that this might entail.

The reader is left to reflect on the narrative possibilities whilst looking at the final cameo picture in which Katy's teddy bear makes his final appearance. But this is not the comforting toy of previous pages. Wearing Sean's joke glasses it presents the reader with a disturbing image, which could be mocking as much as laughing. Browne leaves the reader to decide whether Katy needs to reclaim her childhood comforter, or if she can acknowledge that the changes in her exterior world are mirrored by those in her inner life.

In *The Night Shimmy* Browne's pictures extend Gwen Stauss's written narrative. The book tells of the lonely and shy child Eric and his dependence on the Shimmy to speak for him. Eric is comfortable with his new friend Marcia because she does not demand conversation from him.

The pictures in the book are presented in two contrasting styles. Those which refer to Eric's anxieties are mounted within a thick black border. In their attention to detail, these picture have a photographic-like quality and the white text on the stark black background appears as a caption to the picture.

The pictures in which Eric first meets, and then begins to form a friendship with Marcia have a softer quality and, as Eric begins to conquer his shyness, the black borders disappear and the pictures spread out into a full-plate. The black text appears on the opposite page, surrounded by white space.

The book offers a perfect partnership of words and pictures. The narrative framework is woven out of both. Ahlberg (in Moss 1990, p. 21) has described such texts as ones in which 'you can come out of the words and into the picture and you get this nice kind of antiphonal fugue effect.' The subtleties of the layout in this book add to the narrative contained in the written text and pictures.

Some parts of the book have no need for written text for Browne's use of tone and colour describes Eric's emotion in a way that words could not. The four centre pages are painted in shades of blue. In one picture the reader must go cold and panic with Eric as he searches for the missing Night Shimmy. As Eric peers under the bed he meets the reader's eye. In speaking the words of the text, the reader becomes Eric's Night Shimmy.

The fruitless search for the Shimmy leaves Eric wild with frustration and anger. The quiet of the blue pages is shattered as the noise of Eric destroying his toys is matched by the crack of lightning against an orange sky. No words could adequately describe this for all readers. Each must fill gap in the written text. In doing so, both the adult and the child reader can reflect on the universal need for the comfort of a personal Night Shimmy to help in the conquering of fear and anxiety.

In a small scale research project (Walsh, 1992), I offered a selection of multi-layered picture books by Anthony Browne to children aged five, seven, eleven and fourteen. Working in peer-pairs, the pupils moved towards a joint understanding of one book. This process often necessitated the selection of evidence from the text in order to persuade each other of a point of view. There were occasions where no consensus could be reached or where no satisfactory explanation of an image could be found. In each case the readers brought their own individual personal and social experiences to the task. The study offered a clear illustration of the value of collaborative talk and reading as the pupils negotiated a joint interpretation of the symbols in order to complete the narrative framework.

The narrative framework in the book was the only common factor to the readings, for the pairs of pupils selected different images to focus on, resulting in considerable variations in the interpretation of the text. Each pair was asked to re-read the book at a later date, which in turn offered further unpickings of the layers of meaning and yet more interpretations of the framework.

One of the books selected for use in the study was *The Visitors Who Came To Stay*. In it Browne offers the reader a cyclical narrative framework in which the harmony in Katy's life is upset by the arrival of the visitors and only restored when they eventually leave. For the youngest pair of pupils, aged five, the disruption in Katy's life was symbolised by the expression of alarm on her teddy bear's face when the visitors first enter her home. A reading of the text by the seven year old pupils suggested that the surrealistic images scattered throughout the book were an indication that Katy was dreaming about her future and that once she returned to reality, harmony would be restored.

Much of the reading of both the eleven and fourteen year old pupils focused on Browne's use of colour. One picture depicts Katy and her father on a station platform, looking up the railway track towards a bridge. Whilst the pair stand in a cheerless, wintry scene, the countryside on the other side of the bridge is bathed in summer sunshine. The eleven year old pupils suggested that Katy and her father had moved away from summer into the winter-like environment. For these pupils, Browne was indicating that Katy's past life of contentment was about to end.

The older fourteen year old pupils explored this text for a full hour on their first reading. They made several references to Browne's use of light and shade, suggesting that Katy was shown in shadow whenever she was unhappy. These pupils were the only ones who did not appear to enjoy the humour in the book. Indeed they suggested that Sean, far from being a harmless prankster, was quite a sinister character. The black and white tiled floor in Katy's kitchen was likened to a chess set, complete with a chess piece. This was symbolic of Katy's life which was being taken over by Sean and his mother. Early in the reading, one pupil became convinced that Sean had stolen Katy's teddy bear. For her, the final picture depicting the teddy wearing his joke glasses offered evidence of her theory. The menacing quality of the visitors was confirmed by the final full-plate picture of their house and garden which is filled with an array of confusing images. For these pupils, this page offered a representation of all Katy's horrors during the visitors' stay. This picture acted as a warning that the cyclical pattern was about to begin again, with no happier outcome.

This study revealed that the multi-layered picture book challenged both the inexperienced and mature reader. Although the older pupils sometimes offered a more sophisticated reading, many of the fine details in each text were only noticed by the younger readers.

Everyday life in a western society is filled with an ever increasing range of texts. These are not neutral substances and the reader needs to acquire the necessary skills to be able to respond appropriately to them. The nature of the multi-layered picture book demands that the reader actively read for meaning. The reader enters into a process of co-authorship, interpreting the written and picture text beyond a literal reading.

These apparently simple texts can be interrogated in depth by all readers, resulting in very different realisations of the author's narrative framework. The implication for the teacher and parent must be that such books should be part of the range of texts offered to the Middle and High School pupil as well as the younger First School pupil.

Picture books referred to in this chapter

Browne, A. (1977) *A Walk in the Park*. London: Hamish Hamilton

    (1982) *Bear Goes to Town*. London: Hamish Hamilton

    (1983) *Gorilla*. London: Julia MacRae

    (1984) *Willy the Wimp*. London: Julia MacRae

    (1985) *Willy the Champ*. London: Julia MacRae

    (1986) *Piggybook*. London: Julia MacRae

    (1992) *Zoo*. London: Julia MacRae

Browne, A. & McAfee, A. (1984) *The Visitors who Came to Stay*. London: Julia MacRae

Browne, A. & Strauss, G. (1991) *The Night Shimmy*. London: Julia MacRae

Carroll, L. & Browne, A. (1988) *Alice's Adventures in Wonderland*. London: Julia MacRae

McKee, D. (1980) *Not Now Bernard*. Leicester: Anderson Press

Oram, H. & Kitamura, S. (1986) *In the Attic*. London: Beaver Books.

Chapter Three

Bridging The Great Divide: Picture Books for Children in Secondary Schools

Martin Godleman

One area of curriculum awareness that secondary English teachers are beginning to benefit from thanks to National Curriculum links between Key Stages Two and Three, has been an exposure to what has been going on in local primary schools. Part of the Language In The National Curriculum (LINC) initiative in Sutton schools gave its secondary English teachers the chance to spend days with primary colleagues, and it was at a meeting of language co-ordinators in Sutton that the idea of taking a GCSE class into a primary school first arose. Three schools had shown how their students in Year 2 and Year 3 had written and produced their own picture books (a National Curriculum task), which were then kept in special book boxes in the school library for other children to read. The secondary teachers were made aware of the influx of superb children's picture books in the last ten years, reaching new heights with the sophistication of books like Janet and Allan Ahlberg's *The Jolly Postman*, the brilliant picture and text interplay of David McKee's *Not Now Bernard* and the subtextual illustration craft of Anthony Browne's *A Walk in the Park*. A National Curriculum in English is forcing many colleagues to look at curriculum content from Years 1 to 11, in a way destined perhaps at last to bridge the 'Great Divide' between primary and secondary schooling.

The primary book projects at these primary schools, fired undoubtedly by good teaching and the availability of quality textual exemplars, raised the eyebrows and interests of many secondary teachers at these meetings. Many of them were keen to foster links with schools they all knew the names of, but not much else. Contacts were established to be co-ordinated by the LINC advisory team. The next step was facilitating a genuine curriculum link.

My own school, which was involved with the project in Sutton, currently runs two five-week modules in Years 10 and 11, when GCSE groups are collapsed and staff offer 'module choices' to students. The experience of different teachers, student curriculum choice and achievable short-term goals has made this a successful initiative for students and staff alike. I decided to offer a 'Language and Picture Books' module to this year's Year 10 students, offering them the opportunity to meet the children from a local feeder school and write and publish some picture books to be donated to their library. A short visit to one of our primary feeder schools that had run their own picture book publishing project, set up two mornings for the boys from my school to visit at each end of their module.

The boys who had chosen the module spent their first week looking at the contents of two *Books for Students* bookboxes of picture books The first was aimed at children aged 0–6 and the second for those aged 9–13, and both contained generous helpings of the best available, along with some short readable texts about the writers themselves. I found that most of the students were young enough to have been exposed to some of the better picture books in their own years at primary school, and some had younger brothers and sisters already reading them. It was interesting that the students did not regard the books as 'babyish' or below them, though they had known what they were going to be working on before they selected their option groups. The two bookboxes were brought in by the Primary Language Co-ordinator and the LINC Primary Advisor, who spoke to the group about how the picture books were often used in the primary classroom. In addition to this, several *Janet and John* books were handed round, much to the amusement of the students. The pupils were read a *Janet and John* story from back to front and then from front to back, and asked to guess which was the right way for the story to be read. The lesson was further made poignant by a reading of Wendy Cope's delightful poem 'Reading Scheme'.

On the first visit to the primary school, the students were understandably nervous. The Head spoke to them about the children they would be going to meet, some of whom were in the middle of their Key Stage One National Curriculum Tests, and then took them round to the classrooms. The talk was excitable, many boys commenting on their own primary days and how much things had changed. Two of the group had attended the school themselves and they were, as one of them later confided, 'gobsmacked'. Gifted with a bright sunny day, each boy took two children from Year 1 or 2 classrooms out onto the grass area in front of the school, and read to them from picture books they had brought along from the two bookboxes. One boy had anguished after school with me the previous week over a choice of book for this purpose, asking if he could take a book without any text as he was not confident about his reading. Knowing the boy well and his reading problems, I asked him why he had chosen the module as there was every chance it might involve some reading out loud. He told me quite shamelessly that he was aware he had a reading age of seven, and he thought it might help him if he had the chance to work at reading with children of that age. He eventually chose two 'picture only' books and one that featured some text.

With an hour at the school the boys were able to see up to six children, some of whom read to them from the picture books they had made and written in their own school. It was soon clear to them that these younger children were quite expert in the field of 'reading' picture books, a fact not lost on published writers themselves.

> Younger children see details in pictures much more than adults. If you see them for instance at work with Anthony Browne, they are digging out information that the adults haven't even begun to see. (Aidan Chambers in *The English Magazine* No.17)

All the boys on the module had expressed an interest in visiting the primary school, but it was still quite unexpected to see how well they coped with the children in their care. They all found different strategies to make reading the picture books more successful; asking the children who they were, taking turns, sharing reading, using guessing games, feigning ignorance in order to seek explanation; tactics that teachers of reading of all ages might use. Everyone involved with the project was really excited about the way things had developed; I found myself sitting at the edge of the grass, silently watching what was happening; there was no need for any teacher involvement.

The next time the class met, they had all decided who they were working with and what they were going to write about. They took most of their cues from the published picture book approaches. Some of the subjects they chose to write about were (i) *Wait and See*, the story of a boy whose father is made redundant; (ii) *Terry 4 Tea*, about a boy who liked dressing up as a monster; (iii) *My Hero!* the story of a boy who gets the chance to meet his favourite footballer at a book signing session; (iv) *Stanley*, about a boy who wants to remain bored even though he meets a genie who is prepared to give him three wishes and (v) *No Such Thing as Monsters*, a story about a suburban couple preyed upon by some strange creatures.

The boys generally worked in pairs, some sharing the tasks of writing and illustrating, others taking them individually. There were several resource issues that were difficult to resolve: the kind of paper to write on,

The next day, on his way to school,
Terry walked along with his mates
when

Figure 3.1

what type of print they wanted, whether they would use speech bubbles or not and how to interplay picture with text. Although their Knowledge About Language (KAL) skills did not extend explicitly to the metalanguage of words like 'subtext', 'visual impact' and 'interplay', these were all issues they chose to discuss before any decisions were made about the way a page was to look. One boy remarked that even though it was only being written for six and seven year old kids, what they were doing was much more complicated than redrafting a GCSE essay. Whether it was the novelty of the task, the knowledge that they would have to produce something for their return visit or the joy of writing for an *appreciative* audience, their combined efforts were profound.

Sharing text at the level of writer, reader or illustrator is a process that teaches a great deal about the way language works. Kevin, writer and illustrator of *Terry 4 Tea*, was keen to work the text to create different impacts on the reader. Having developed his main character Danny, a quiet schoolboy who loves dressing up as a monster at home, but who is bullied at school, he introduces the monster. Danny meets the monster, but refuses to be frightened by him and in the end befriends him and tells him about Terry, the bully. By this time the reader, who was perhaps at first confused that a story called *Terry 4 Tea* has a main character called Danny, will be making predictions about Terry, now it is clear he is the bully. Will he be eaten up by the monster or invited to tea by Danny? Kevin works the text to the turn of the page (figure 3.1): 'The next day, on his way to school, Terry walked along with his mates when . . .' (Reader turns page) 'Aaaaaarrrgggghhhhhhhh!' (figure 3.2). The monster arrives, causing Terry and his friends some degree of consternation. This is about the closest the written text can get to simulating a visual shock, interplaying the effect with the picture of the monster on the next page. Terry's friends think they've realised the monster is Danny dressing up; the reader shares the writer's knowledge that this is not Danny. What will happen now? The next page (figure 3.3) shows the monster, slightly fatter, with no sign of Terry and friends other than a shoed calf, bitten off at the knee. Kevin has omitted to draw the fact that they've been eaten – the story is developed through the implication of the conclusion. As far as the rest of the story goes, the monster explodes on the next page and Danny is later seen on his way to school, never to be troubled again. Kevin was certainly influenced by the picture book he had read, *A Halloween Mask for Monster* by Virginia Muelley, but what he had managed to achieve with the picture book he had produced, demonstrated a sophistication somewhat belied by the Ds he had been achieving in his written work at GCSE.

Other stories developed with a similar sense of experimentation, all lessons now devoted to getting out the 'workfiles' and begging round the

"AAAAAARRRRGGGGHHHHHHHHH!"
Terry and his mates jumped.

Figure 3.2

Monster was full, so full that

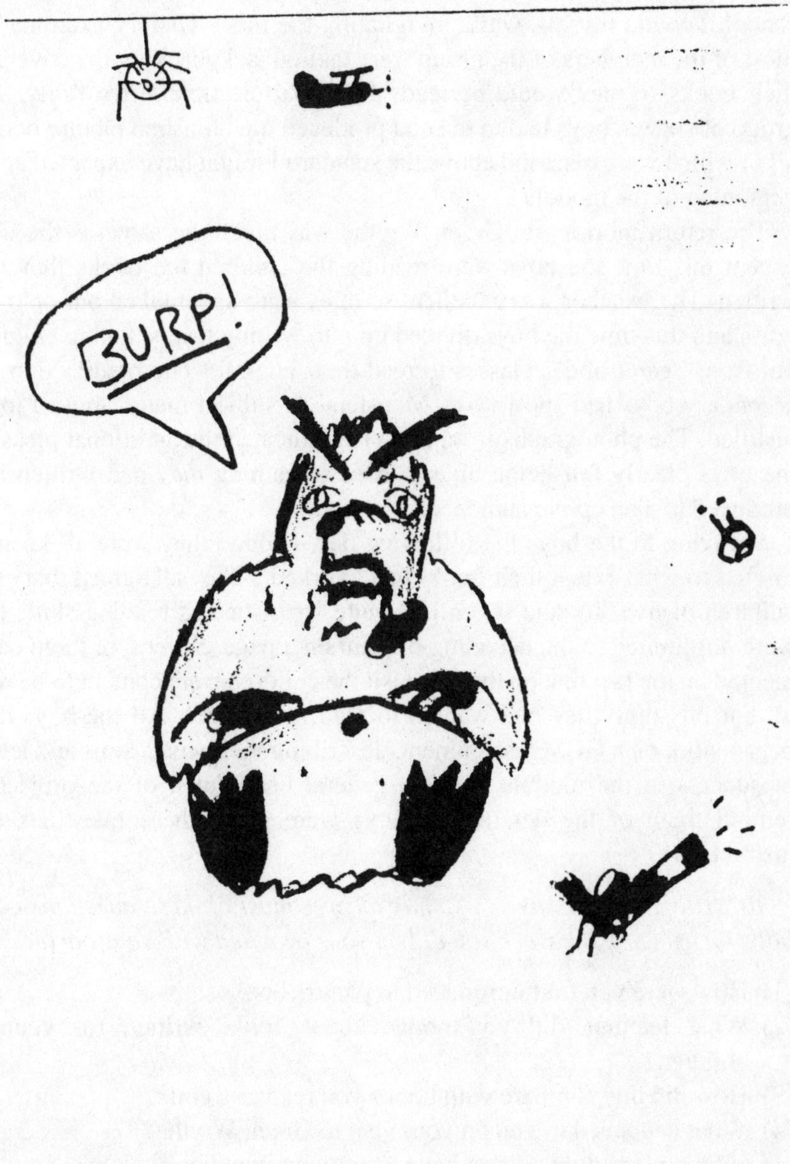

Figure 3.3

other departments for coloured pencils, scissors, prittstick, tackyback, HB pencils, erasers and so on. After several experiments with print enlargements and computer printer fonts, the boys decided to write up what they wanted in print, page by page, to have it enlarged on the photocopier and stick it underneath the picture it referred to. The effect was quite pleasing, but the group were rapidly running out of time. It was a rewarding but time-consuming process. On the morning of the return visit to the primary school, I found myself, while invigilating the mock History examination most of the members of the group were taking, tackybacking the covers of their books so they would be ready for departure time at ten-thirty. The group of sixteen boys had in the end produced nine finished picture books, all of which were over and above the standard I might have expected at the beginning of the module.

The return morning at Green Wrythe was much the same as the first, except this time the boys were reading the children the books they had written. The weather was excellent so mats were again taken out onto the grass and this time the boys divided up into writing teams, taking children out from Year 1 and 2 classes to read their book to. The predilection the secondary boys had shown for 'Monsters' as subject matter looked to be justified. The photographs from this visit indicated the additional pleasure the boys clearly felt being able to read something *they* had written and produced to a receptive audience.

Speaking to the boys the following day, I found they were all keen to discuss to what extent their books had 'worked'. They all agreed that even children of five, six and seven had quite sophisticated reading skills that were not limited to the decoding of print on a page. Several of them commented on the fact that on the first visit the children were content to be read to, but this time they had wanted to read themselves. All the boys then began work on a GCSE assignment, describing their work, aims and levels of success in the module. After a general breakdown of the project to remind them of the details, the boys were given these questions and instructions:

To write a good essay . . . simply answer most of these questions carefully, focusing on the work you did on your own and with your partner/s.

(1) How were you first introduced to picture books?
(2) What features did you notice about books written for younger children?
(3) How did this compare with books you read as a child?
(4) What happened to you on your visit to Green Wrythe?
(5) What plans did you first have about your own book?
(6) What kind of decisions did you make as you wrote it?

(7) What problems did you come up against in putting your book together and how did you get round them?

(8) What pleased you/displeased you about the final product?

(9) What happened to you when you took your book to Green Wrythe?

(10) What have you learned about reading/English/books/anything else from this module?

(11) What advice would you give those doing it next year?

The written responses to these questions showed the extent of the exercise's potential to develop Knowledge about Language skills in these four-teen year olds in terms of writing, reading and speaking:

> . . . the books have to be exciting and there has to be something in the book for them. There may be something true or realistic, like going to bed early, but not 'There's mummy, there's daddy; Daddy goes to work . . . ' and so on.

> The features I noticed about the picture books were the attractive pictures. Big colourful pictures make a child want to look at a book. Big text was also another important part. The books were not too long, but had enough in them to keep the reader occupied for some time. We had to get this balance right too.

> I kept thinking when I looked at the page about how I would use my eyes if I were a 5–7 year old.

These visits had been something which had shown everyone who had taken part how sharing reading and writing can be a genuinely pleasurable and educational experience, in addition to providing a wealth of material with which to discuss KAL. On the strength of the experiences gained on our two visits, three of the boys had gone on to ask the Head at the primary school if they could work there for their one week Work Experience placement in July.

The final touch was to give each boy a colour photocopy of the picture book he helped put together to put in his GCSE folder along with the module assignment. The original books themselves were presented to the children's library at the primary school after the summer break.

There were several reasons why this project developed ideas about language for all those concerned with it. As far as the primary students were concerned, they had seen themselves as real writers in the context of a genuine 'outside' audience, involved in the creation of books for themselves through their own efforts as writers. They were also able to see themselves involved in a learning experience with other students, contributing ideas that were central to the creation of the new picture books. At the presentation assembly, much was made of the primary students' efforts in the process, the books being presented to representatives from their groups.

As for the secondary students, they had been given the opportunity to see themselves as teachers of all stages of the writing process from the germ of an idea for a story to the reading of the final printed page in front of a captive and *known* audience. They had could now appreciate the complexities of the picture book with its multifaceted interactions between picture and text. Several of them commented on the 'teaching' they had done, and none of them, it seemed to me, would ever see themselves as 'learners' in quite the same way again. Giving students the opportunity to see themselves operating in a teaching environment, controlling the synthesis of ideas, process and structure through to the establishment of a final product was invaluable in their understanding of how language develops; in a world freer from assessment pressures, time might more frequently permit such curriculum forays to encourage an understanding that learning is not just about facts and product, but process, too.

My perception of myself as a facilitator of language development changed, too. This was a project that on many occasions reduced my 'teaching' role to photocopier and resource officer; the inevitable implications for students learning from behind the curriculum steering wheel are fascinating. I saw that primary children were just as competent at identifying and successfully managing the processes of writing as secondary pupils; with children a few years older than them, they performed with greater confidence. The language barriers were reduced, and the children were somehow freed to work on the writing process with less inhibition and a clearer focus for audience through task. Treating these children as experts in their own field raised expectation and removed the enforced
failure other more traditional language exercises often proliferate. I was reminded of Richard Knott's comments in his book about English Departments:

> ... children learn by making meaning through language, through the reading, writing, talking and listening they are engaged in. The overlap between these modes of language is continuous and the learning is most effective when the children are most actively engaged. (*The English Department in a Changing World*, Richard Knott, OUP, p. 26)

Harnessing such projects across 'the Great Divide' has implications for Language Policy documents. There is now a move to look more specifically at the many reading, writing and talk processes children have been involved in at primary school. A larger and more detailed 'language record' can be built up by reference to such language experiences, giving a more comprehensive picture of each individual child's language development. The degree to which our secondary schools can build on this kind of information may, of course, be greatly influenced by the role (and assessment value) of Knowledge about Language in the English National Curriculum. Nevertheless, the Project made a strong case for an equal

Curriculum. Nevertheless, the Project made a strong case for an equal valuation of process and product where language development is concerned, for children of all ages.

Special thanks are due to Sheila Wooldridge and the staff and children of Green Wrythe Primary School for their enthusiasm and participation in the project.

Chapter Four

Such Agreeable Friends: Children and Animal Literature

Pat Pinsent

> Animals are such agreeable friends – they ask no questions, they pass no criticisms.
>
> (George Eliot, *Mr. Gilfil's Love Story*)

Anyone spending a few minutes browsing among children's books in a bookshop or library will have no doubt of the enormous popularity of animal characters. From *Spot* pop-ups to pony books for teenagers, the variety and abundance of such books must transcend those in all other similarly broad categories. Why are these books so popular with writers, teachers, parents and especially with children themselves? How much do children's choices of particular types of animal books reflect their age or stage of development?

Fantasy Literature for Children

Nearly all animal literature is a branch of fantasy, a form which while not peculiar to children's literature is more frequent in it than in much of adult reading. In the Introduction I have cited writers who emphasise the importance of narrative fiction as part of children's reading, but fantasy perhaps needs some additional justification, since some adults fear that it, more than the rest of children's literature, is 'merely escapism'. This in itself may not, of course, be such a bad thing!

I would however like to argue that fantasy is far more important than this – that it is, in a kind of way, 'truer' than much so-called realism. Books which never depart from what is theoretically possible may for instance imply that defeating evil forces is not too difficult for a determined band of children. Some semi-documentary books for children may go beyond this and appear to claim that if everybody knew all about other people's customs the whole world would automatically become tolerant and heaven on earth would be established. Since fantasy doesn't claim to be about the 'real' world, there is less danger that it will indulge in these kinds of falsifications. What fantasy says is not limited by 'facts', so there is greater freedom to speak at more depth.

Fantasy literature for children takes a variety of forms. Much of it is set in other worlds, whether of the past, out in space or reached through some kind of 'door' from our world. Most animal books, however, are set in a version of our world. There are significant exceptions to this, like the *Alice* books and the *Narnia* books, but while both of these have important animal characters, I would argue that they are not truly animal books as such, for the focus is so strongly on the human characters. In most of the animal books ostensibly set in our world, the world is however changed, enabling non-human animals to speak, think like humans, interact with other species which often include human beings, and frequently perform feats which are, as far as we know, beyond them.

I have no intention of setting up a hierarchy and claiming that realism is inferior to fantasy, for children need books of all kinds, those set in our world as we know it just as much as those which take place in 'impossible' other worlds. Nevertheless, I would claim that there is an important role in young children's development for books set in a changed version of this world. For one thing, it is 'safer' than a totally imaginary secondary world, for there is no fear that the character with whom the child is identifying may not get back home. At the same time, it is also more secure than the too realistic book which can be frightening because of the similarity of its setting to the world known by the child. The kind of world which resembles ours except that in it the animals can speak is a good context for a child's exploration of concepts and emotions.

The Adult's Role

One of the reasons for the widespread sales of animal stories aimed at the youngest children is undoubtedly the way in which they are enjoyed by the adults who are reading to the children. Waterland (in ed. Styles et al., 1992) describes a 'multi-layered' book as one which 'has new things to think about and new things to appreciate whenever the reader chooses to read it.' Clearly such a book, even if read many times by an adult, will still provide enjoyment, and will create what Watson (op. cit., 1992) terms:

a special kind of irony: the adult narrator and the adult bedtime reader exchange a knowing and solemn look above the head of the listening child. But the child . . . *is* listening.

I would claim that the best animal books for children are indeed multi-layered in this sense. Such books are likely to evoke in the adult a more complex response than in the child, partly because the many echoes of earlier readings of this and other books and all their life experiences may enrich the current reading. This complexity is especially likely to occur in the case of humour, where the adult can see many allusions of which the child is unaware. A well-known instance of this is in A.A. Milne's *Winnie the Pooh*:

> 'Good morning, Pooh Bear,' said Eeyore gloomily. 'If it is a good morning,' he said. 'Which I doubt,' said he.
> 'Why, what's the matter?'
> 'Nothing, Pooh Bear, nothing. We can't all, and some of us don't. That's all there is to it.'
> 'Can't all *what*?' said Pooh, rubbing his nose.
> 'Gaiety. Song-and-dance. Here we go round the mulberry bush.'
> 'Oh!' said Pooh. He thought for a long time, and then asked,
> 'What mulberry bush is that?' (Chapter 6)

The characterisation of Eeyore, the dissonance between the literal and metaphorical understandings, the accurate evocation of speech, the deliberate pausing, all are likely to be a source of humour for the adult, while the child listener, and later reader, may start from a simple enjoyment of association with Pooh and gradually, with increasing maturity and awareness of other people's characters and conversation, grow into a fuller understanding of Milne's meanings.

A Scale of Anthropomorphism

I would argue that there is a scale of anthropomorphism in animal books which to a considerable extent parallels children's psychological development. Such a categorisation is in no way rigid; books defy any classification and can be enjoyed at different stages, especially if presented by an adult who enjoys them. My main point is that, generally, the more anthropomorphic the characterisation of the animals, the younger the age group that will normally enjoy the book. This does not, however, apply to fables, or books like *Animal Farm* where the author has a clear polemic purpose directed towards adult readers.

A. BOOKS FOR THE YOUNGEST CHILDREN

The animals in books for the youngest readers and listeners frequently justify their description as 'ourselves in fur' (quoted in J.R. Townsend, 1976) rather than being realistic portrayals of non-human creatures. Quite often, of course, the animals might more accurately be described as toys (as in *Winnie the Pooh* and *Dear Teddy Robinson*). Species interrelate with complete abandon, and no language problems exist, either between each other or with humans. They have human emotions, and their distinctive animal characteristics are at the most superficial level. They often wear clothes (as with Peter Rabbit's jacket and Paddington's hat) and have no particular difficulties about using human artefacts (*The Tiger who Came to Tea*).

Part of the reason for the continued popularity of these books is clearly wish fulfilment – children want to believe that they can talk to their pets and toys; they associate these with the ones in the books, which are generally cuddly. These animals thus satisfy the child's need for something or someone who combines the warmth of a kindly adult with an element of being controlled by the child. The popularity of animals which seem most to resemble humans, like Teddy Bears, has been accounted for by Tudge (1989) in terms of the human need to understand other human beings:

> Because we are so alert to others of our own kind, we also have especial sympathy for creatures that in some way seem to resemble us. We like animals that walk upright, as we do: penguins and bears. We like animals that manipulate: monkeys and squirrels and elephants . . . we imbue all the things that touch our lives, including other animals, with attributes that 'make sense' of what we see . . .

I would like to argue, however, that there are additional reasons why animals like these answer particularly to the needs of the very young child. Children need to validate and legitimate their own experience by identifying with others who have had similar experiences and emotions. They need, at one and the same time, to share the weaknesses and ignorance of a character, and to feel superior in knowledge and strength to that same character. Books which allow them to do this certainly include *Winnie the Pooh*. More recent examples are *The Owl who was Afraid of the Dark* by Jill Tomlinson and Dick King-Smith's *The Hodgeheg*. In the latter, little Max is searching for a safe way to cross the road, and the children will be way ahead of him when he at last finds a school crossing lady to help him. In the meanwhile, they will have empathised with his vulnerability, his inability to do things on his own and his tendency to get words mixed up, which incidentally provides humour at their level. When his family commiserate with him after an accident:

'I got a head on the bump,' he said slowly.
The family looked at one another.
'Something bot me on the hittom,' said Max, 'and then I headed my bang. My ache bads headly.'

Perhaps it is a little surprising that a character as uncuddly as a hedgehog should be endearing, though his shape is otherwise quite similar to the human form. In a book like this, the child identifies with the character and yet stands back from it at the same time. It could be said that in such books the child is combining the roles of Parent and Child – being strong and weak, greedy and at the same time capable of realising that greediness is naughty, being fearful and yet above the fear, being baby and grown-up (like Christopher Robin). Animal fiction fulfils this function better than books which only have child characters, because it is easier for the child reader or listener to associate with *and* dissociate from the characters at the same time. As Thwaite (1990) suggests:

> The listening or reading child recognises himself in Pooh and recognises himself as he longs to be, as he thinks he *will* be, in Christopher Robin. (p. 301)

Appleyard (1990) in his exploration of the developmental stages in reading fiction from childhood to adulthood, defines five roles which readers take. The first of these is 'Reader as player'; listening to stories allows children to possess a fantasy world which they learn to control. Books like those mentioned above allow the child to have this kind of control.

Another function which animals can perform for the young child is to allow for the existence of internal monsters. This seems to be achieved more easily within the fantasy framework than the existence of a very naughty child character by itself might allow. Sendak's Max, in *Where The Wild Things Are,* has it in his own power to go to the land of the monsters, control them by the force of his stare, and leave them when he chooses to do so. There is clearly no need to explain this most Jungian of texts to a child – its symbolic value can be implicitly appreciated at a very young age. Other kinds of monsters, especially wolves, abound in fairytales and provide a pleasing and safe kind of catharsis. I think, however, it is important not to be speciesist – children need bad characters but wolves and rats shouldn't always be typecast. The occasional *good* monster, wolf or rat character can assist the child in accepting some of the sides of their personality which are more difficult to control.

B. Young Readers

Not all highly anthropomorphic books are appreopriate for the youngest children; exceptions such as Hoban's *The Mouse and his Child* spring readily to mind. But it seems to me that, as the age of the intended *child* audience increases (I'm assuming throughout that at this stage there will also be an *adult* audience), there is a tendency for the animal characters to have a few more of the qualities of their species. Animals in these books usually still have the ability to communicate directly with humans and members of other species, but the reader is more aware of them as non-human, sometimes because the author makes a point of reinforcing their species qualities. In *A Pet for Mrs. Arbuckle* a special emphasis is in fact laid on some of the qualities of the potential pets:

> 'I'd be a stimulating pet,' said the giraffe.
> 'I could see over the fence and tell you what was happening next door.'
> 'I'd like that,' said Mrs Arbuckle.
> 'But look at it this way,' argued the gingernut cat.
> 'Do you want all the tops of your trees eaten off?'
> 'No, I suppose not,' said Mrs Arbuckle.

We have here again an instance of a multi-layered text; the adult reader may particularly enjoy the fact that while all the potential pets claim positive qualities, the cat (who, we quickly realise, itself wants the job of pet) reminds Mrs. Arbuckle of their negative ones. The child reader is likely to be led towards this understanding and to predict the happy ending.

The child considered here, in the lower and middle part of the primary school, could be seen, in terms of the stages described by Appleyard (1990), as in transition between the 'Reader as Player' role described above and 'Reader as Hero/Heroine'. At the latter stage, Appleyard suggests that children become central figures in their developing construct of the world, and relish stories which help them explore their role. The children I am considering here are really in transition between these two stages. They may not be ready, perhaps, for the more challenging adventure stories which are popular amongst those at the fully fledged 'hero/heroine' role stage, but they need to be able to try things out, to experiment – to be at the centre of their own story, yet to be able to disown the story when it becomes inappropriate to their requirements. They particularly need characters to identify with. They are often prepared to change the details of stories to suit their needs. After a reading of *Gobbolino: The Witch's Cat* to a mixed class, I found that the girls' stories either changed the gender of the central character to female, or made his sister Sootica, far more central to their writing than he was in Williams' book or, indeed, in the stories of the boys.

The process of trying to understand how people's minds work, as well as one's own, extends to trying out what it would be like to be an animal. An interesting example of this process is to be found in Ahlberg's *Woof*, about a boy who periodically changes into being a dog. This is described lightheartedly, but clearly introduces an element of suspense which might be too stressful for a child younger than those considered here. Will Eric be stuck as a dog forever? It provides an opportunity for the child reader to experience vicariously both what it might be like to be an animal, and also to have some understanding, in a small way, of a sense of loss – both of human qualities when Eric is a dog, but also of canine attributes when he reverts to boyhood. A similar 'game' is played in Paul Gallico's *Jennie*, ostensibly a book for an older reader or even an adult. Though this book would be demanding reading for many children, it is not unduly sophisticated, as the central character is a boy of eight who becomes a cat, an idea not beyond the young child, especially if being read to.

The idea of fantasy providing a means of dealing with a sense of loss is explored by M. and M. Rustin (1987), who suggest that it provides a way of coping with emotions which in a realistic framework might be too difficult for a child to handle. They include in their discussion a number of important animal books, including Pearce's *A Dog so Small* and *Bubble and Squeak*, White's *Charlotte's Web*, and Hoban's *The Mouse and his Child*. Books like these, however potentially distressing the loss concerned might be, treat it in a way which ultimately offers reconcilation rather than abandonment. I would argue that the process is made all the more accessible to the child through the animal-fantasy element.

C. ADVENTURE

The second of Appleyard's (1990) stages, that of the child being hero/heroine of their own adventures, seems particularly appropriate to animal books, as they afford the opportunity for the child to identify with an adult (since the animals usually are adults) in a way they probably wouldn't so readily be able to do in real life. Thus children can have more interesting adventures. The animals in the books appropriate to this stage often live mainly with members of their own species, though sometimes they can communicate with other animals (seldom with humans). Richard Adams' *Watership Down* is particularly relevant here, and Robert O'Brien's *Mrs Frisby and the Rats of NIMH*. The animals' thought processes are recognisably human, but the author has often gone to a good deal of trouble to make sure their life style is recongisably animal.

Some animal adventure books go one stage further away from direct anthropomorphism, by never allowing their animal characters to speak, even to members of their own species, but nevertheless, experiencing thought processes which are seen from the inside, and which seem to be of a human type. They may, like the female cat called Lord Gort, in Westall's *Blitzcat*, have superhuman powers, but the reader is well aware that they are animals. To some extent, as well as identifying with adult characters, such books make it easier for readers to suspend their disbelief. The level of powers required by the rabbits in *Watership Down* and the amount of coincidence in *Blitzcat* are easier to accept in a less realistic mode than they would be in a totally realistic genre (our defences are already down). Many of these books again treat with loss – of friends, relatives – a familiarising with death, in a way which isn't so threatening as it would be in a totally human setting – many children's first acquaintance with bereavement is inevitably with the loss of a pet. The use of cats, dogs and rabbits as central characters may not be entirely fortuitous here either.

Books like these often leave the young reader with the sense that more is meant than appears at first reading, a quality which is likely to make them want to reread the book. Authors, whether intentionally or not, often use this form to say something about the human condition under the guise of animal behaviour, another instance of such books being multi-layered. Adams, for instance, as well as clearly making judgments about acceptable forms of human society, admits (1974) that he incorporated his ideas about leadership in *Watership Down*, without having realised at the time that he was doing so.

D. 'REAL' ANIMALS

The least anthropomorphic animal books are those where the child in the story projects human feelings on to an animal, usually a pet, without the animal itself being apparently any more 'human' than the pets which might belong to the readers. In Montgomery's *Foxy*, Estes' *Ginger Pye*, and Pearce's *A Dog so Small*, for instance, there are children with an intense longing for a pet, which eventually results in a relationship with an animal. In *A Dog so Small*, this longing goes so far as to make the central character, Ben, indulge in the fantasy of a make-believe dog, but more usually, the child pet owners simply see their animals as superior to others of the species. The focus is usually on a human child – who can be the 'adult' to the animal, teaching, training, being a sourse of strength for it. This allows the child reader, often on the verge of adolescence by the time they reach such books, to play with qualities like nurturing. Books which are popular at this stage, such as those about girls owning ponies, are not necessarily more subtle, and may often be less well written, than those for younger children, but they clearly fulfil an emotional need.

Appleyard (1990) suggests that the adolescent looks to stories to discover insights into the meaning of life, and authentic role models. This may not of course always be done through quality literature, and young people of this age often need a good deal of 'pulp' reading. The kind of animal book which allows for adventure, this time with the human in a leading role, perhaps in wild territories (as in some of Jack London's books) can fulfil this need, though adventure stories with animals in leading roles are by no means excluded. Whatever the rest of the reading diet at this point, it is likely that animal books, if still enjoyed, will be much less explicitly anthropomorphic than those read earlier.

I do not see these stages of anthropomorphism and children's development that I have suggested as in any way 'watertight', and books which from some points of view might seem to imply a younger audience can well be very demanding and make the older reader look at them for hidden meanings. The fact that the protagonists in Hoban's *The Mouse and his Child* are toys, the mix of the species and the intercommunication between them might lead to classifying this complex book as being appropriate to younger readers than would find it readily accessible. Even so, it does have an appeal to children who are quite unaware of some of the issues which Hoban explores, such as the question of the possible meaninglessness of life (even though this suggestion appears to be rejected in the reconciliation with which the book concludes).

Other Aspects

Children – and their teachers and parents – seem to know instinctively the value of animal books. The fact that authors continue writing them and that they are published, reflects this to some extent – clearly, what is popular is likely to be published. But I think there are other reasons why authors are drawn to write in this genre. Of course, there's their own experience as children which leads them to write for the child in themselves. Often, too they write as parents or relatives for specific children, as the lives of Kenneth Grahame, A.A. Milne, Beatrix Potter and many others prove.

There are however other factors. Books with animal protagonists avoid awkward questions – about age (the characters can, as mentioned above, do adult things) or race. I have the impression that more animal picture books are being produced than ever before, partly because in a multi-ethnic, multi-cultural society, they avoid difficulties, and may even, like David McKee's *Tusk Tusk*, be used to preach toleration.

Occasional sparingly used 'typical' qualities can help young children understand character. This kind of device is probably most acceptable at the most anthropomorphic stage. The kinds of greed exemplified in *Winnie the Pooh* and *The Tiger Who Came to Tea*, or the typical behaviour of the animals (and children) in *Mr Gumpy's Outing* make for humour, as long as stereotypes are later challenged, for instance by the mice and rats in *Mrs. Frisby*.

Perhaps particularly attractive today, to both readers and writers, is the way in which animals can seem closer to nature than humans are. The ecological emphasis can be a means of making us not only understand more, but empathise more about, for example, loss of natural habitat as in *Watership Down*.

It would be wrong, however, to be over didactic in advocating animal literature for children. The advantages must come first and foremost from the enjoyment which the children experience in them. My intention rather is to reinforce this enjoyment, to legitimate the reading of material which children, teachers and parents have always found stimulating and in a kind of way, bonding. Animals *are* 'agreeable friends'; we can project our own emotions on to them much more safely than we can on fellow humans, we can detach ourselves from these emotions when we need to much more easily than from humans – as George Eliot says, 'They ask no questions, they pass no criticisms'.

Children's Books discussed in this chapter

(Most of the editions listed are paperbacks, even when there exists an earlier hardback edition)
Adams, R. (1973) *Watership Down*. Harmondsworth: Penguin
Ahlberg, A. (1987) *Woof*. Harmondsworth: Penguin
Bond, M. (1962) *A Bear Called Paddington*. Harmondsworth: Penguin
Burningham, J. (1978) *Mr. Gumpy's Outing*. Harmondsworth: Penguin
Estes, E. (1969) *Ginger Pye*. Harmondsworth: Penguin
Gallico, P. (1963) *Jennie*. Harmondsworth: Penguin
Hill, E. (1989) *Spot's Baby Sister*. London: Heinemann
Hines, B. (1969) *Kes*. Harmondsworth: Penguin
Hoban, R. (1976) *The Mouse and his Child*. Harmondsworth: Penguin
Kerr, K. (1968) *The Tiger Who Came to Tea*. London: Collins
King-Smith, D. (1989) *The Hodgeheg*. Harmondsworth: Penguin
McKee, D. (1978) *Tusk Tusk*. London: Andersen
Milne, A.A. (1926) *Winnie the Pooh*. London: Methuen
Montgomery, J. (1971) *Foxy*. London: Pan
O'Brien, R. (1975) *Mrs Frisby and the Rats of NIMH*. Harmondsworth: Penguin
Pearce, P. (1964) *A Dog so Small*. Harmondsworth: Penguin
Robinson, J.G. (1966) *Dear Teddy Robinson*. Harmondsworth: Penguin
Sendak, M. (1970) *Where the Wild Things are*. Harmondsworth: Penguin
Sewell, A. (1954) *Black Beauty*. Harmondsworth: Penguin
Smyth, G. & James, A. (1989) *A Pet for Mrs. Arbuckle*. Harmondsworth: Penguin

44

Tomlinson, J. (1968) *The Owl Who was Afraid of the Dark*. Harmondsworth: Penguin

Westall, R. (1990) *Blitzcat*. London: Pan

Williams, U.M. (1965) *Gobbolino: the Witch's Cat*. Harmondsworth: Penguin

Chapter Five

Making Connections: Children's Books and Cohesion

Barbara Hearn

> look
> here it is
> in here
> it is in here
> no it is not in here
> where is it?
> can you help?
> we can help you
> look . . .

Perhaps you recognise this extract from an early book of a well known reading scheme. What sort of a story does the text tell? In fact the book is called *the egg* (sic) and the illustrations reveal that it is about a magician hiding an egg in different places. However, even with the aid of attractive illustrations the story can hardly said to engage young readers. When I shared this book with a group of four year olds they did not recognise the main character as a magician and the concept of a man doing magic tricks with an egg seemed beyond their experience.

I have quoted the book as it is written, without capital letters or full stops. Each line is written on a different page. None of the characters are named and the egg is always referred to as 'it'. The text resembles a dialogue but the reader is given no indication that this is so. The word 'here' is difficult for young children to understand as it relates to the location of the speaker, who we infer is the magician. The text as a whole is disjointed and there is no cohesion.

Why is the text written in this way? The aim of the reading scheme is to make the task of learning to read easier. This leads to the creation of a text with short sentences, a restricted vocabulary of simple words, and the removal of capital letters and full stops. The ensuing language produced is stilted and unnatural, making the reader's task of making sense of the text harder than when natural language is used.

In written language, meanings are created by the complex relationships between words. Hunter-Grundin (1979) explains this:

> Words in themselves have often very little meaning, but when words are put together into sentences they take on meaning from each other, so that the meaning of the sentence is something more than the 'sum' of meanings of individual words. And when sentences are put together into a meaningful and interesting story, each sentence takes on a more specific and clear meaning as part of the story. In this way a meaningful context is created, and this context provides cues that are vital to the reader. (p.77)

Cohesion

This interconnectivity of words, as described above, is referred to as the 'cohesion' of the text. Cohesion is not something that we are explicitly aware of; we have an implicit knowledge of how these structures work but are not conscious of the cognitive processes involved in understanding them. Some of these implicit relationships between words require the reader to connect words that can be separated by several sentences.

The reading process requires that readers become involved with texts and interact with them to gain meaning. In essence, reading is about making sense of writing; it involves the interpretation of written symbols in order to recreate the author's message. If we knew how texts conveyed meaning then we might gain insight into what is involved in the reading process. The new science of text linguistics has been making headway in gaining such insights.

The work of Halliday and Hasan (1976) has been prominent in the field of text linguistics. They drew attention to units of text larger than a sentence and the interconnectivity involved. They describe what it is that creates cohesion of a text, and examine the actual words and phrases that help the text hang together. Chapman (1983) followed up the work of Halliday and Hasan, saying that it has 'great potential for helping teachers to appreciate what is involved in the reading process.' (p.4)

When reading, we make sense of the whole text, connecting items from earlier parts of the text to the part presently being read. We don't make sense of each sentence independently and then put these meanings together. The meaning of one element, a word, phrase, clause, or paragraph cannot be understood in isolation as the meanings of different items are usually interconnected. Nearly every sentence contains elements presupposing others.

Even very simple stories for young children make use of cohesion. In order to understand such stories children have to make the correct connections between the sentences to retrieve the global meaning of the story. Chapman (1987) investigated children's development of the perception of cohesion and found that the ability to perceive and process cohesive ties is associated with reading proficiency and comprehending. The full understanding of pronouns in written texts is still developing as late as ten or twelve years of age. (p.43)

The term cohesion refers to the unity of a text within itself; it is the linguistic explanation of interconnectivity, that is, how a text hangs together. To give an analogy I would like to suggest that cohesion provides the skeleton of a text, supporting the meaning and providing structures for words to be attached in order to create a unified whole.

Chapman (1983) has taken up the work of Halliday and Hasan and in his book *Reading Development and Cohesion* he indicates the centrality of the 'cohesive tie', a term used for the connection between two textual elements such that the latter element relies on the former for its full interpretation. Most cohesive ties work across sentence boundaries and contribute to the overall cohesion of the text by giving it unity or global quality.

An example of two sentences showing simple cohesive ties would be:

Peter went to the shops.
He bought some biscuits for his mother.

In this example the two cohesive ties, 'He' and 'his' in the second sentence are connected to 'Peter' in the first sentence. 'He' and 'his' are both examples of 'anaphora', or backward acting cues. Readers need to interpret the relationship between items such as these in order to fully comprehend the words they read.

Cohesive ties give a text semantic integration and are usually assembled in 'chains' which interweave through a text. These chains create text unity and enable tracking of characters, objects and events. Below is a simple example of 'chaining':

Susie ran down to the sandpit with
her bucket and spade. She started to
dig in the soft yellow sand.

In this example the words 'Susie/her/she' form a chain about Susie. However, there is another cohesive chain running through this short text. The second chain is based on the semantic links between the words 'sandpit/bucket/spade/dig/sand'. All of these words are associated with one another and can be said to 'collocate'.

Collocation, one of two categories of lexical cohesion as identified by

Halliday and Hasan (1976), occurs when words that are associated with one another are used, for example a well known pair of words that collocate are 'fish and chips'. However, the association does not have to be this close for the words used in a text to be said to collocate. The second category of lexical cohesion is reiteration, which occurs when words are repeated. These may be the exact words or synonyms.

Among other types of cohesive ties are conjunctions which operate by linking one idea in a text to another, and pronouns, one of those most frequently found. They are usually used to refer back to a named person or thing, so tying two parts of the text together. Third person pronouns such as 'he', 'she', 'they', are easier for a reader to understand than first and second person pronouns such as 'I', 'you', 'we', which are more typical of speech.

Cohesion and Texts for Children

In order to assist young children make sense of written language, the stories they are introduced to should be cohesive. When cohesion is lacking, as demonstrated by the reading scheme book, it is very difficult for the reader to make sense of the text. In a research project I conducted (1992) I investigated the cohesive ties in the books used by reception classes in two schools, one class using a published reading scheme, the other class using story books. I aimed to compare the differences, if any, between the two sets of books. I was undecided as to which were the most suitable materials to use for beginner readers and hoped that my investigation would provide some objective information.

Teachers are very aware of the need to present learners with attractive materials that will engage their interest. However, they also feel the need to ensure that the children receive some structure in the materials used for reading. Many teachers are concerned that when using story books there may not be enough repetition to enable readers to acquire a basic sight vocabulary. The findings of my research show that story books can be used to provide all the requirements necessary to produce fluent readers.

To carry out my investigation I took the twenty most frequently read books from each class. I analysed the books using the categories of cohesion described in Chapman (1983). The findings revealing the most differences are given in figure 5.1:

	Reading Scheme Books	Story books
Pronouns (Personal references)	385	220
Words like 'here' (demonstrative references)	124	15
Conjunctions	23	89
Reiteration	227	263
Collocation	49	302
Sentence length	4.02	6.3

Figure 5.1

The category 'collocation' shows the largest variation of any between the two sets of books. In the story books one in every seven words collocates with another whereas the ratio for the reading scheme books is 1:41. This shows the limited use of collocation in the reading scheme books, where there are only 49 instances of collocation in total. In these books the collocations are usually in pairs of ideas; for example in the book *butterfly* (sic) the following sentences are repeatedly used:

> where is it?
> look here it is

In this extract the words that collocate, 'where' and 'here' do not add to the interest of the text.

In contrast, every story book makes use of collocation, and there are a total of 302 collocations. The latter often occur in long chains of associated words which create cohesion by connecting different parts of the text. The following example, taken from *Gregory's Garden*, a text of a similar level to that of *butterfly* (sic), is typical of the story books in that there are several different chains of collocation running through the text:

> Gregory dug the soil.
> The birds ate the worms and beetles.
> Gregory planted the seeds.
> The birds ate them up.
> Some of the seeds grew.

In this extract there are three or more chains of collocation. The first chain is 'dug'/'soil'/'worms'/'beetles'. This is followed by 'birds ate'/'worms'/ 'beetles'/'seeds'. The third chain is 'dug'/'soil'/'planted'/'seeds'/'grew'. These chains of collocation overlap and interweave to form a web of meaning and make the text a cohesive whole.

The other category of lexical cohesion, reiteration of the same word did not reveal any marked differences between the reading scheme books and the story books. I had assumed that the reading scheme books would contain more reiteration than the story books as the main aim of the reading scheme books was to reinforce the core vocabulary. However, the reverse was true and I found slightly more instances of reiteration in the story books. Some of the story books used reiteration in a very creative way to construct cohesive texts which maintained interest. The reading scheme books did not achieve this, since most of the reiterations were of a rather uninteresting, bland nature as shown by one of the reading scheme texts *where is it?* (sic):

> where is it?
> it is not in my home
> can I help you look?
> it is not in my home
> can I help you look?
> it is not in my home
> can I help you look?
> we can look here
> it is not in my home
> where is it?
> look here it is
> I can help look
> here it is look look look

However, when we look at a story book of a similar length, which contains a similar amount of reiteration, the complete text is full of interest, as shown below in *A Halloween Mask for Monster*:

> It was Halloween.
> Monster tried on a girl mask.
> "Too scary," Monster said.
> Monster tried on a boy mask.
> "Too scary," Monster said.
> Monster tried on a dog mask.
> "Too scary," Monster said.
> Monster tried on a cat mask.
> "Too scary," Monster said.
> Monster looked in the mirror.
> He saw his own face,
> "Just right," Monster said.

The story books rarely make use of words such as 'this' and 'here' whereas the reading scheme books use the word 'here' a great deal. In the early reading books the word 'here' occurs once every eight words. As the reading scheme books progress, fewer demonstratives are used. Demonstratives such as 'here' are typical of speech, the word 'here' referring to the location of the speaker's immediate surroundings. This makes them very hard for young children to understand in writing. The early reading scheme books do not use speech marks nor do they use speech signifiers such as 'said'. The text is left to stand without any context other than the pictures and the reader is left to infer where the 'here' is located. This makes the text rather disjointed and non-cohesive.

There are nearly four times as many conjunctions in the story books (89) compared to the reading scheme books (23) which only use two conjunctions 'and' (additive) and 'but' (adversative). The story books use eight different conjunctions representing all four categories: additive, adversative, causal and temporal. This adds to the richness and diversity of language used as well as making the story books more cohesive.

Of all the findings the personal references (pronouns) are the most complex to analyse. This is because many of the pronouns used in the early reading scheme books do not refer to a named character and thus are non-cohesive. Indeed many of the these books do not give names for the main characters; pronouns are used on their own. An example is shown below from *Come for a ride*:

> Can I go out to play, Mum?
> Can I go for a ride?
> Yes, you can
> but play in the park.
> Let's ride down here.
> No let's ride down here.
> We can go fast here...

As shown in this example, the pronouns 'I', 'you' and 'we' are first and second person pronouns which create a text resembling speech. Out of the total 385 pronouns in the reading scheme books, 285 are first and second person pronouns compared to 86 first and second person pronouns used in the story books. The story books use more third person pronouns such as 'he', 'she', 'they' etc. which refer back to named characters. This is demonstrated by the following excerpt from *Happy Birthday Sam*:

> It was Sam's birthday.
> He was a whole year older.
> He climbed out of bed
> to see if he could turn
> the light on all by himself,
> but he still couldn't reach the switch.

There are only six reading scheme books which contain true cohesive ties using pronouns. The majority of these ties involve the pronoun 'it' as seen in *My Home*:

> Where is my home?
> Is it in here?
> No, not here.
> Is it in here?
> No, not here.

The text repeats the last two lines four more times and the word 'it' is repeated eight times, always referring back to the word 'home' in the opening sentence. The word 'he' is only used a total of five times in the reading scheme books.

A completely different picture is seen in the story books. Seventeen of the twenty books contain cohesive ties using pronouns. Of these, ten have only third person pronouns and those which use first and second person pronouns often identify the speaker. Thus the pronouns form cohesive ties and the pronouns can be connected to named references as shown by the following excerpt from *Noisy Nora*:

> Jack needed burping,
> So Nora had to wait.
> First she banged the window,
> Then she slammed the door,
> Then she dropped her sister's
> marbles on the kitchen floor.
> "Quiet!" said her father.
> "Hush!" said her mum.
> "Nora!" said her sister,
> "Why are you so dumb?"

In this excerpt the reader can identify that the 'she' and 'her' refer to 'Nora' which helps to connect different parts of the text to make it cohesive.

The Implications of these Findings

The findings indicate that the reading scheme books use a specific register which is unique to these books. It consists of a pseudo-dialogue which uses many pronouns but does not name the characters, leaving the reader to infer who is saying what from the illustrations. In addition the word 'here' is used a great deal in the early books which makes the text even harder to understand. The reader is often unable to find the exact location for 'here' as it changes according to the speaker. Other linguistic features include frequent repetition of the same word, very little collocation and short truncated sentences, all of which make the texts non-cohesive.

The story books use a wide range of registers. The main linguistic features of story books are that they all use chains of collocating words and a wide variety of conjunctions. Most use pronouns which refer to named characters and signalling devices to show when a character is talking. These features ensure that the texts are cohesive and have a global quality.

The meanings of the story book texts are far more accessible to young readers than the reading scheme books. This is rather ironic as the reading scheme books have been written with the intention of making learning to read easier. If we take the tenet that learning to read is about making sense of texts then the reading scheme books would appear to make the task harder than story books which have been written for children's enjoyment.

My research reveals that the use of a restricted vocabulary in the reading scheme books causes problems because words are omitted which then have to be inferred in order to comprehend the texts fully. This view is supported by Clay (1991) who warns against texts that are 'contrived to emphasize sounds or words'. She advises that:

> Attempts to control texts and learning sequences in these ways have probably made the learning task more difficult because important support systems within the language have been left out. (p.187)

The reading scheme books use a pseudo-dialogue, which when presented in a written form causes difficulties not encountered in genuine dialogues where the context and audience are present. To make sense of these texts the young reader has to combine cues from a variety of sources, the printed text, the pictures and an understanding of how spoken language operates.

The story books, on the other hand, are exclusively concerned with communicating meanings to their readers. There is no restriction of vocabulary and the context is made explicit as the author's aim is to construct a meaningful story for children. The authors use a variety of registers, making use of a range of cohesive structures. It is interesting to note that the story books contain slightly more reiteration than the reading scheme books. The argument that reading scheme books give the learner more practice at reading the same words does not have any validity. This is especially true if beginner readers are encouraged to return to favourite books again and again.

Many of the registers of story books will be familiar to young readers if they have been read to. There is a natural continuity of progress if children move from listening to stories read to them to reading the stories by themselves, with a gradual withdrawal of adult support. No such continuity exists when the texts have a specific register only encountered in reading scheme books.

Before I started my research I was undecided as to which reading materials were the most suitable for beginner readers. I used an eclectic approach, combining ideas from the 'real book' approach with the use of a published reading scheme. However, on completing the research I would now favour the use of story books.

Suggestions for Choosing Texts for Beginner Readers

There are several features of books that help young children make sense of written texts.

1 The most important feature is that the book contains an interesting or amusing story that will engage readers and help sustain them through any difficulties encountered within the text.
2 There should be more than a single line of text on each page to help readers make the connections between the different parts of the text, to gain complete understanding.
3 Characters should be named to help make the story explicit.
4 Where pronouns are used these should be close to the referent so that beginner readers can connect the two easily. Preferably pronouns should be in the third person e.g. 'he', 'she', 'it', 'they'.
5 If speech is used there should be clear signifiers of who is saying what. Speech bubbles make this explicit in books for very young children. As readers mature the use of speech marks and words such as 'said', 'shouted' etc help provide the context needed for full understanding.
6 Reiteration is very helpful for beginner readers by providing plenty of practice in reading the same words. Many story books for young children make use of reiteration in a rhythmical, aesthetically pleasing way.
7 Finally, if the book is meaningful to young readers and provides a pleasurable experience they will want to return to the text and reread it. Frequent rereading of favourite texts is an excellent way to attain fluency.

Children's books referred to in this chapter

READING SCHEME BOOKS

Ginn 360 A Selection of Level 1 and 2 books: 1978 – Core Readers; 1983 – Little Books. Aylesbury: Ginn & Co. Ltd.

STORY BOOKS

Hutchins, P. (1982) *Happy Birthday Sam* (Picture Puffin) Harmondsworth: Penguin Books
Mueller, V. (1986) *A Halloween Mask for Monster* (Picture Puffin) Harmondsworth: Penguin Books
Stobbs, W. (1984) *Gregory's Garden*. Oxford: Oxford University Press
Wells, R. (1978) *Noisy Nora*. (Picture Lions) London: Collins

PART TWO : THE READER

Chapter Six

'Once upon a time': A Study of Children's Response to Fairytale

Susan Fremantle

'Do you know any more like that, Miss?' asked a ten year old boy in an inner city school, of the student who had just told the class the story of Cinderella. Daily for a week she told similar tales: 'Red Riding Hood', 'Sleeping Beauty' . . . to a wide-eyed group of top junior children who, almost unbelievably, knew none of them and hung on every word. The children's librarian at my local public library reports that fairy tales are among the most frequently borrowed books, yet other students and teachers have told me, 'Children these days don't seem to enjoy fairy tales. They think they're babyish.'

Fairy Tales and Young Children's Thinking

My own childhood, in a period lacking the variety of children's books available today, was filled with stories from the Bible, myths, legends, and above all, folk and fairy tales. They provided entertainment, escapism and a moral and idealistic dimension to a rather circumscribed and solitary childhood, and the characters of books became playmates and role models. Characters like Andersen's 'Little Mermaid' and 'Little Match Girl' presumably embodied feelings of loneliness and alienation which at that stage I could not express for myself.

All readers are familiar with the 'that's me' feeling which comes from a story reflecting their own experience. Fairy tales accomplish this with their universal themes, just as powerfully as any more realistic story, but with greater safety, since the fairy tale, being unlocalised in time and place, need not be recognised by the reader if it is too threatening to do so.

Fairy tales are ideally suited to young children's thinking. To them the 'real' world and the fairy tale world are both morally coherent places, where the good are rewarded and the bad punished. Indeed the fairy tale world, for all its dangerous beasts and evil characters, is frequently more predictable than the 'real' world where (in the child's eyes) justice is often inexplicably absent. As both the moral chaos and the unpredictable nature of justice gradually impinge upon children, they have an increasing need to find within themselves a moral paradigm which remains clear and immutable, upon which to base their thinking and their actions. The wisdom and morality of parents will eventually be questioned and rebelled against, but the moral values laid down by fairytale and myth may enter the subconscious via the emotions of the reader, and provide a strong foundation against which there is no need to argue or rebel. (Compare the response to story by the children described by Mary Walsh in Chapter 14).

The child of six to eight does not observe the story as a whole, weigh up who acted morally and then resolve to follow their example. A logical and abstract process like this would be quite beyond the capability of such a young child. According to Bettelheim (1976), the young listener makes an emotional identification with the hero [or heroine] who struggles to overcome various tribulations. The listener struggles alongside the hero, sharing his suffering and eventual triumph. The qualities and values of the hero are thus emotionally imprinted upon children and unconsciously form part of their value system.

Many traditional stories are concerned with the very ordinary, even inadequate individual (often symbolically represented by small size or low intellect) who struggles to survive against life's odds (represented by dangerous quests or threatening creatures). The success of the hero or heroine offers the similarly small and ineffectual child-listener a message of hope and encouragement that they too will succeed in life. The story provides images which structure the listener's thoughts and imagination in new ways, opening up fresh possibilities for interpretations both of past events and for future actions. What children have not imaginatively identified themselves with Cinderella, Hansel and Gretel, or Jack (of the Beanstalk), thereby discovering more about their ability to cope with life with patience, bravery or cunning? Of course, all literature offers the readers 'images to think with' (Chambers, 1984, p.172), but perhaps no other kind does it so clearly and effectively as do fairy tales. This is possibly their most important feature. The patterns found within these stories are mostly clearly defined and easily detected by the child listener, and they are clothed in a narrative and linguistic style which is easily understood and remembered, provided care is taken to match the story version with the needs of the particular audience. Thus these tales offer the child 'images' with a power unrivalled in children's literature and at an age (approximately six to nine) when children are perhaps at their most impressionable.

An Investigation into Children's Response to Fairytales

I have no doubt about the lasting influence upon my own development, both emotionally and morally, of the Bible stories, folk and fairy tales, and myths and legends, which occupied a substantial part of my life between the ages of six and ten. Whether it is possible to find evidence of such influence upon today's children was one of the questions which prompted me to undertake a small research project. Because of limitations of space, it is only possible here to highlight a few of the findings of this project.

Because of the contradictory opinions about children's enjoyment of fairy tales, which I quoted at the beginning of the chapter, my first objective in this research was simply to observe the degree of enjoyment which children found in the experience of a wide variety of folk and fairy stories, a list of which is appended at the end of this chapter. A number of children aged seven and eight, from three schools of different socio-economic make-up, rural and suburban, were observed in both mixed and single-sex age-based groups for one session per week over a period of approximately six weeks. There was ample time to get fully acquainted with the children, who enthusiastically welcomed my visits. As there was also time to overcome any initial over-excitement or competitiveness, the results are unlikely to have been seriously distorted by factors related to the research situation.

All the discussions with the children were taped, and at the schools' suggestion, the children will be similarly followed up in a year's time to investigate any changes in their response to fairy tales. Close analysis of the tapes brought to my notice many points which I either did not observe during the sessions, or else interpreted incorrectly at the time – a valuable lesson for anyone engaged in research on children's response.

1. UNEXPECTED RESPONSES

While there was no doubt whatever about the children's enjoyment of virtually all the material used in the sessions, the stories were not always enjoyed for the reasons an adult might expect. A book might be greatly appreciated for one particular incident within the story, or even for a special picture. An example of the latter was the troll in 'The Three Billy Goats Gruff', yet it later emerged that the *whole* story had not in fact been fully understood. The height of the mattresses in 'The Princess and the

Pea' was of far more interest to the seven year olds than the fact that 'she was a real princess' who because of this quality, lived happily ever after. The eight year olds, however, retained a far greater sense of the story as a whole and were less distracted by its parts.

Similar distractions occurred, especially among the Sevens with *The Paper Bag Princess*. The princess cunningly outwits the dragon and rescues Prince Ronald, only to cancel their engagement when he rudely criticises her grubby appearance because she is dressed in a paper bag, the result of the loss of her clothes from the dragon's fire. The Eights generally understood and enjoyed the humour of the role reversal and the pastiche of a traditional 'prince rescues princess' fairy tale. However, the Sevens were unable to comprehend the story patterns; the ending was 'wrong', and one child insisted 'they probably got married next week'. Others hardly noticed the ending at all. Their attention was caught early on by the dragon's incineration of fifty forests, and an animated discussion ensued as to the best way of preventing a dragon from breathing out fire. 'Take him to the river. Jump in the river and swim away, and the dragon jumps in the river to get you,' [presumably extinguishing the fire]. 'The fire would go out if she put water in his mouth'; '. . . water all over his body'; 'Put a rope round his neck and choke him and fire can't come out.'

While there were many indications of enjoyment of the story, it was probably not for the reasons intended by the author. That adult presenters of a story should endeavour to match the content and language to their audience's conceptual and linguistic capabilities goes without saying. What the children bring to a story, however, by way of their own interests and knowledge of the world and of other books, determines what they get from it. Children will take from any story those ideas and feelings which they are capable of receiving.

How far should the adult endeavour to ensure that children 'get the point' of a story? I found that when I had to explain the ending of a story ('The Three Noodles' to the Sevens, 'The Selfish Giant' to the Eights) their satisfaction and enjoyment was far less than when they either 'got it' spontaneously or worked it out for themselves.

2. INACCURATE INTERPRETATIONS

Should the adult explain the details to children, in order to ensure that they take the 'right' message from a story, for in fairy tales pattern and moral are as important as the characters and events? Or should children be allowed to take whatever they can or want, irrespective of its 'correctness', provided they are enjoying themselves?

Problems could arise if an incompletely understood story were to be the basis for future tasks or if other stories were going to be built upon it. Partially inaccurate and distorted interpretations were far more prevalent than I had been aware of during the actual sessions and were only revealed by careful analysis of the tapes. A busy teacher would almost certainly miss them. The misapprehensions that arose were seldom linked to the language of the stories; they stemmed from a more profound inability to see the patterns made by the narrative and to understand how this particular genre works (see Meek, 1988). Sometimes difficulties resulted from an inability to accept the pattern or ending, again, owing to an unfamiliarity with fairy-tale conventions, or to an over readiness to apply rules from the children's own 'real world' inappropriately to the secondary world of fairy-tale.

The importance of this issue stems from the influence that Bettelheim (1976) and others believe that fairy-tale has in the development of the child, something I would endorse from my own experience. If the patterns and messages of the tales are to imprint morality upon children and to offer hope that 'if one does not shy away but steadfastly meets unexpected and often unjust hardships, one masters all obstacles and at the end emerges victorious' (Bettelheim, p.8), then it is obviously vital that the true messages and patterns of the tales are communicated to the child without omission or distortion.

3. REALITY AND FANTASY

The root of the problem is in the young child's initial inability to distinguish between reality and fantasy. Seven is usually considered to be the age at which fairy tales can safely be introduced, without the children being afraid that the dark events and characters of the story may 'really' enter their own lives. Yet even the most mature and literate of the Eights at times asked questions or passed comments that were quite inappropriate to the make-believe world of the fairy tale. The dragon's fiery (and smoky) breath was greeted with a horrified 'That's polluting!'. And the wolf's consumption of Red Riding Hood's grandmother produced. 'I don't understand. When the wolf has eaten Grandma and she's all in pieces, how can she come back to normal and with her dress on?' (This comment referred to J. Goodall's wordless picture book version of the tale, 1988).

'It's too thick round his neck' said another eight year old when the child in 'The Selfish Giant' threw his arms round his neck and kissed him. 'How come the giant [in this story] grew old and died but the Sleeping Beauty slept for a hundred years and never grew any older?' was yet another unanswerable question.

Some of these older children could understand and accept my answer about the picture in 'Red Riding Hood': 'you can't ask that sort of question; it's a fairy tale.' Others could not. Some of the Sevens made comments showing equally blurred boundaries between the real and the fantastic and were even unsure if they themselves had ever seen trolls ('Billy Goats Gruff'). 'There is trolls in this park,' said one. I asked, 'Which park?' 'I forget now. When my sister was a baby, she's fourteen now, it was true then.' It is interesting to compare the research discussed by Applebee (1978) into the beliefs about fairy tales expressed by five and six year old children.

Yet the same children also stated about 'Tom Thumb': 'It's a fairy tale. Tom Thumb won't get killed.' And about 'Little Dog Turpie', who is dismembered and then put together again without ill effects, they said, 'It's a folk tale. It's not real!'

The obvious conclusion is that there is no precise point in a child's life when reality and fantasy are clearly distinguished. This understanding dawns gradually, with many steps, some of them regressive. Appreciation of this uneven development is needed by adults both for their selection of suitable material for children and for their efforts to detect where hindrances to full comprehension may lie. For a child needs ultimately to be able to enter the secondary world of each individual fairy tale, detect the rules which operate within that particular world, and to feel in control and comfortable within it. Such imaginative projection into the 'safe' world of the fairy tale is an essential precursor to the willingness and ability to project into the lives of others which they will need as adults in the far more dangerous 'real' world – imperative if we are to live harmoniously alongside our neighbours.

Children's Strategies in Understanding

The children themselves coped very efficiently with any difficulties in understanding they might have. They never asked for explanations of language. They simply filled any gaps from their own imaginations and such story patterns as they were familiar with. The Sevens could not cope with the role reversal of 'The Paper Bag Princess' nor with the ending 'and they didn't get married after all', for it did not have the necessary neat tying of loose ends required at this age. They simply ignored the ending, declaring 'Oh poor her!' and 'Maybe after a couple of weeks they might marry each other.' Even after I had emphasised Ronald's rude and ungrateful behaviour and Elizabeth's pleasure at being free to 'do her own thing', it was still thought that maybe they would marry when they grew up! In contrast the Eights had no problems with either the role reversals or the ending. *All* agreed with Elizabeth's rejection of Ronald, the girls being especially appreciative of her command of the situation and right to choose. Yet paradoxically, some simultaneously thought that it should be Ronald's right to decide if they should marry – an indication perhaps of confusion between the traditional and more modern perceptions of a woman's role. The whole subject of the rights of women in fact produced a wealth of material which sadly cannot be dealt with here.

The Children's Appreciation of Pattern and Symbolism

It quickly became obvious in the sessions (doubly confirmed in the tape analysis) that those children with the greatest knowledge of fairy and folk tale were better able to understand new tales, and to get greater satisfaction from them than those children less well acquainted. Enjoyment seemed to lie predominantly in two factors: the actual events of the story – the 'what happened next' aspect; and the recognition of patterns involved. This latter quality was indicated by an ability to predict ahead with reasonable accuracy.

The attention of the younger children was chiefly engaged by the 'what happens next' factor. They seldom gave much impression of enjoying the pattern, with two notable exceptions. The first was 'Grandpa and the Magic Barrel', in which anything that fell into the barrel re-emerged in quantity, starting with a gold coin and ending with a vast number of identical Grandpas! This completely delighted them, and would have easily stimulated dramatic, written and artistic responses had time permitted. The other story was 'The White Cat', in which the King's third son is triumphant in his quest for the most beautiful bride when he brings home a white cat whom he truly loves and who turns out to be a bewitched princess. This also contained several patterns predicted accurately to their great satisfaction. It is worth noting that this was the last story of the project, and their skills had greatly improved. Had the story been read earlier on, they would probably have been much less able to appreciate the patterns.

The older children were pattern hunting almost from the outset of the research. All the children, whatever their age, became very much more proficient with practice. Their enjoyment increased with their proficiency and did not decrease with over exposure either to me or to fairy tales as I had feared. All the children read both visual and verbal clues with far greater accuracy by the end of the research, and the Eights also attempted interpretation of Anthony Browne's *Hansel and Gretel* where frequent use is made of pictorial symbolism. This had varying degrees of success, with marked differences between children, but overall, considerable improvement was made within the course of reading the one book. The group were offered *Dear Mili* (Sendak) immediately afterwards and at once applied their newly acquired skills, not altogether appropriately, but to their own obvious delight and satisfaction. For me it was a salutary lesson that even quite young children can acquire an apparently 'literary' skill, and enjoy exercising it both for the sense of power it gives them and for the light it sheds on a text. In addition, once learnt it was automatically transferred to another situation without further adult intervention.

Two further essentials for the enjoyment and patterning need to be mentioned. Pictures not only provided vital clues to meaning, but stimulated their own inner 'picture making'. Some stories had no pictures and there was scope for the formation of individual visual images uninfluenced by another's vision. But in some cases illustrations in a book were found wanting in comparison with those in their imagination, indicating their confidence in their own right to create freely.

Time also was needed in abundance to allow the children to tell anecdotes (at times apparently very tenuously related to the tale) or to recall an alternative version, or even other stories which were perhaps similar in pattern. Such space for the children's contribution was essential in order for them to establish their own active involvement with the narrative. While it was sometimes lengthy, it did not distract them overall from the story being told. The other tales recalled often indicated how the children had acquired a vague sense of the pattern of the story. Through their telling of their own similar anecdotes they were able to engage more closely with the basic pattern.

Conclusions

That the children enjoyed the wide variety of folk and fairy tales is beyond doubt. The more I read, the more they appreciated them. There is a need for sheer quantity, particularly for those less familiar with the genre. I have earlier voiced my concerns that distorted messages and patterns may be absorbed through only partial comprehension of a story, and I found detailed explanations were only partly successful in rectifying this. In addition, too much explanation is distracting and inappropriately pedagogical in what should be a relaxing and enjoyable shared experience. Enthusiasm is best caught, not taught, and the teacher's own enjoyment is an important part of this. One very interested teacher of the Sevens started reading Hans Andersen to her whole class with most appreciative responses. I would have thought Andersen to be too difficult linguistically, and too emotionally demanding, but her own and the children's enjoyment was a salutory reminder of the role that enthusiasm can play, and also the fact that children will usually take what they can at their own level and ignore what is beyond them. A sensitive teacher can do much to support children when they are stretched emotionally. It is as dangerous to be over-protective as it is to be over-demanding.

While it is important that the deeper levels of fairy tales reach the listeners' subconscious and pattern their future thinking, my study shows that quantity and familiarity *by themselves* do much to promote the children's further understanding. The children clearly improved their comprehension and their ability to interpret and predict, the more they heard stories and discussed them. An adult can be an invaluable facilitator of discussion, but this must never degenerate into adult-dominated questioning with the children searching solely for the 'right' answer.

Their delight in pattern-finding was perhaps the main pleasure and surprise of this research, and the value of this attribute is obvious. Patterns perceived in one circumstance may enhance the ability to find patterns in other circumstances, be it in another discipline, such as maths or science, or in life itself. In the discussions, the children taught each other about the patterns they had found. My role was almost solely to make space for all to contribute and, from time to time, to pause and ask: 'What do you think is going to happen next?', sometimes followed by 'Why do you think so?' These two invaluable questions promote speculation and invite it to be supported with evidence based upon the text, upon the children's own knowledge and experience of how the 'real world' and its people function, and upon their understanding of other stories and genres. I contributed my own speculations and predictions on an equal footing, not always getting it 'right', but unobtrusively demonstrating the kind of thinking required.

While the children's interest in and use of pattern does not of course *prove* Bettelheim's theories on how fairytale works on the unconscious, it does go some way towards indicating the important role that pattern in narrative may play in children's thinking. If the patterns and images of one story are so readily transferred to other stories, it is surely likely that they may be internalised to form part of the inner store of patterns available to the individual to process the events and experiences daily encountered in the 'real world'.

The negative views on fairy-tale outlined in my introduction may, I suggest, be due to difficulties with a language and style not always accessible to today's children. My groups were of mixed ability and ethnic background. It was essential that all the children could understand the tales, so language and style had to be both easy to comprehend and linguistically interesting. Fairy tale material needs careful consideration by the presenter, for many versions are old-fashioned and over-flowery for today's children; others, in an effort to be more accessible, are unfortunately linguistically boring and banal. Fairytale benefits from a style which communicates its 'other world' atmosphere, but not to the point of incomprehensibility. It was time-consuming to search out exactly the right material, but matching the needs of the children to the level of the book is essential. Otherwise the response will be 'It's boring!' – a term which covers a multitude of negative aspects which children have no ability to formulate more precisely. The list appended here includes versions which seemed to strike the right balance between being comprehensible and yet linguistically interesting and imaginative. Were I to work longer with these children, I would want to present linguistically harder versions of the same stories, since comparing versions was another source of pleasure and introduced the notion of the oral tradition with no single 'right' mode. This would also encourage the children to experiment with their own written and dramatised interpretations; already being familiar with a simple version gives the necessary security to do this.

One final question remains. Would the children have equally enjoyed stories concerned with the daily lives of children like themselves? Many such stories are greatly appreciated by children between six and nine, but fairy-tale and fantasy offer a very different sort of satisfaction. Stories of everyday life may validate the children's daily experiences, and extend their horizons into unfamiliar though related areas. But 'realistic' literature for this age cannot deal with the deeper, less tangible side of life. To write explicitly about the kinds of values, themes and emotions treated in fairy-tales is to make them too hard for children of this age to understand. Yet children have an innate need to engage with the intangible, and the fairy-tale can act as an accessible metaphor for things not yet intellectually understood. From fairy tale, children gain a sense of the magical, the mystical, and the awe-inspiring. Such themes 'cross boundaries of culture, language and age group and seem to reflect the very nature of *homo sapiens* in story form' (Benton and Fox, 1985, p. 38). And at the same time, fairy tales are simply very good fun! Fantasy is concerned with other worlds into which children may escape from the pressures of daily life. Every experience is open to them, but safely so, their imaginations are kindled, and their confidence restored. The children can be triumphant heroes and heroines in every adventure, and who can want more than that?

Folk and fairy tales used in the study

Berg, L. (1966) *Folk Tales for Reading and Telling*. London: Hodder & Stoughton

Browne, A. (1986) *Hansel & Gretel*. London: Methuen

Chambers, A. (1976) 'The Three Noodles', in *Funny Folk*. London: Heinemann

Galdone, P. (1987) *The Three Billy Goats Gruff*. London: Heinemann

Goodall, J. (1988) *Little Red Riding Hood*. London: Andre Deutsch

Jaffrey, M. (1987) 'The Serpent King', in *Seasons of Splendour*. Harmondsworth: Penguin

Le Caln, E. (1973) *The White Cat*. London: Faber

Lurie, A. (1980) 'The Black Geese', in *Clever Gretchen and Other Forgotten Tales*. London: Heinmann

Manning-Sanders, R. (1962) 'Jack and the Beanstalk', in *A Book of Giants* London: Methuen

Manning-Sanders, R. (1976) *Fox Tales*. London: Methuen

Manning-Sanders, R. (1974) *Grandad and the Magic Band*. London: Methuen

Mayne, W. (1980) *The Mouse and the Egg*. London: Julia MacRae Books

Moore, I. (1986) 'The Princess and the Pea', in *The Flying Trunk and Others Stories*. London: Andersen Press

Munsch, R. (1982) *The Paper Bag Princess*. London: Scholastic Publications

Sendak, M. (1988) *Dear Mili*. London: Viking Kestrel

The Tiger and the Rabbit. London: Save the Children Fund and Macmillan Books

Wilde, O. (1978) *The Selfish Giant*. London: Kaye and Ward

Chapter Seven

'The Perfect Ending to the Perfect Story': The appeal of Enid Blyton

Fiona Collins

Enid Blyton, the most prolific of children's writers, is still popular with children today. She wrote about six hundred books, which were published from before the Second World War until her death in 1968 and they are very much in print today. However, it has been said that no other children's author has attracted so much criticism as Enid Blyton. She is seen to be sexist, racist and classist and teachers, librarians and parents alike have also expressed concern about the quality of her writing. The librarians' attitudes have received most publicity, with allegations that her language is hackneyed and repetitive and her characters stereotypical. Because of this, Blyton's books were banned from various libraries in the 1960s and 1970s; Cedric Cullingford (1979) stated:

> They are banned in many libraries, and in some countries banned altogether. Enid Blyton has been accused of being racialist, class-conscious and dominated by the ethics of materialism.

An example of stereotyping occurs in *Five Run Away Together*, where the five children are living in a cave on Kirrin Island. They are all very happy and as usual the weather is lovely. As the children sit having their breakfast, arrangements are made for the day:

> 'Let's arrange everything very nicely in the cave,' said Anne, who was the tidi-est of the four, and always liked to play at 'houses' if she could. 'This should be our home. We'll make four proper beds. And we'll each have our own place to sit in. And we'll arrange everything tidily on that big stone shelf there. It might have been made for us!'
> 'We'll leave Anne to play "houses" by herself,' said George, who was longing

to stretch her legs again. 'We'll go and get some heather for beds. And oh! – what about one of us keeping a watch on the old wreck, to see who comes there?'

In this extract Anne is given the stereotypical female role of home maker. By playing at 'houses' she is internalising the role set out for her by the society of the period. At the same time her peers have the freedom to explore the island. Even George is treated as a surrogate boy. But as J.A. Appleyard (1990) states, popular fiction reflects what is happening at the time in society; it does not try to change or attack these values. When Blyton was writing, girls were seen as being merely domestic creatures.

However, since the 1970s a more positive view has been taken of Blyton's works as a result of her continued popularity amongst young readers. Her books are seen as actually helping children to achieve fluency in reading, showing the child what reading is all about: the ability to lose oneself in the narrative and to become part of the story.

Interested in the appeal of Enid Blyton adventure books, I recently carried out a small survey with a class of ten and eleven year olds in a school in Southfields, SW London. Out of twenty nine children asked, twenty had read Blyton; thirteen thought that she was 'okay', five thought she was 'good' and one 'boring'. None of them thought she was 'rubbish' and none of them thought that she was 'brilliant' (these were the options available to them). When asked why they had read her the answers were in the same mould as this from Claire:

> I just read them because I was given them. I don't think I would have read them otherwise.

The children seemed to be given the books by their older brothers or sisters, a parent or a relative. Often grandparents had kept their own children's books safely in the loft for the next generation of Blyton readers. As Zoë said:

> My Mum introduced me to Enid Blyton, she said that she read them as a child.

It was interesting that the children keep on reading these books which propound values not in tune with the 1990s. It is understandable that a child might read one Blyton book because they were given it by a relative but the children I spoke to had read a great many. As Charles Sarland (1983) points out, the Blyton adventure books are read by audiences far wider than middle class children living in rural settings. A colleague of mine once met two Turkish Moslem girls in a Hackney Primary School who read nothing but Enid Blyton. Her appeal seems to cross class, race, gender and language boundaries. She gives the reader something which stimulates their urge to read. Thus there must have been something else to encourage the children to read through all the Secret Seven or the Famous Five series.

What Type of Reader?

Talking to the ten and eleven year olds in SW London it did seem that the children who read Enid Blyton fitted into a particular category, that of inexperienced readers who wanted more than a picture book, were ready for longer, more complex narratives, but were not ready for such children's writers as Nina Bawden or Betsy Byars. This seemed to be a stage that the children went through, as indicated by the fact that eleven out of the twenty children I spoke to had stopped reading Blyton altogether, while the rest still read her occasionally, in accordance with their reading ability. As Frank Smith (1978) states:

> Children learn to read by reading. Therefore the only way to facilitate their learning to read is to make reading easy for them.

This is what Blyton manages to do and through this she draws the children into the narrative. She opens the door into the reality of escapism where the reader leaves his/her own life behind and joins the Famous Five or Secret Seven for an adventure.

Anne Fine, the children's author, at a conference in 1992 on children's literature at Oxford Polytechnic, told the story of her daughter's introduction to Enid Blyton. Fine and her family were on their way back from Los Angeles to Edinburgh when they stopped at her mother's house in London. The mother presented her grand-daughter, aged seven, with a box of children's books, Blyton included. Before they reached the M1 the daughter had started to read aloud a Famous Five to the rest of the car, commenting on the sexist attitudes but carrying on reading. Fine said that when her daughter got into the car she could read the words on the page but when she got out at Edinburgh she was a reader, she had lost herself in the narrative, had filled the gaps and knew what the enjoyment of reading was. Blyton thus turned Fine's daughter from a decoder into a 'real' reader. If a child feels comfortable with the Blyton style they will have many titles to choose from and each time they pick up a Blyton novel they will have practice at being a 'real' reader. As with everything in life, 'practice makes perfect'.

What is the Key to the Blyton Appeal?

The Famous Five and the Secret Seven series all keep to a particular format and this gives the reader a sense of familiarity and security. The books are unmistakeable; each has a distinctive cover with a title, Enid Blyton's signature and a picture on the front. Inside the cover there is always a small paragraph about the story, the number of the adventure, along with a list of chapter headings:

Five Go To Smuggler's Top
The FAMOUS FIVE are Julian, Dick, George (Georgina by rights), Anne, and Timothy the dog.
If Uncle Quentin had had the top-heavy ash tree lopped, the gale would not have brought it crashing down on to Kirrin Cottage, and then the Five would not have gone to Smuggler's Top to stay with Sooty Lenoir and his eccentric father.
But once there, queer and highly suspicious things seemed to happen, one after the other. Timmy, too, had his fair share of excitement in and out of underground passages, and on the surrounding sea-marshes.
This is the Five's fourth adventure.

The short description of the story supports the readers while reading the story. It also encourages them to read another in the series. Numbering each book acts as a reminder that there are many in the series and allows readers to check which books they have read without having to remember the title. The table of contents with the explicit chapter headings gives the reader an idea of the development of the story, along with providing support as they read. As the reader finishes one chapter the next heading signals what is going to happen, as well as clearly acting as a marker as to where they are in the story.

Both series also keep the same characters throughout. In twenty one of the Famous Five books the characters do not change, develop or age, even though the books were written over a period of twenty one years from the first in 1942, *Five on a Treasure Island* to the last in 1963, *Five are Together Again*. The characters, two boys, two girls and a dog, are always the same age, going to the same schools, living in the same period. The security of reading such a series, knowing there is more to come and that the format is always the same is very reassuring for the reader. J.A. Appleyard (1990) says:

> Repetitive reading of these stories (Blyton, Nancy Drew) is a clue to their attraction. Not only is one book very much like another in the series, but the true fan may reread the same book 'at least a dozen times'. (p.85)

The genre of the adventure/mystery encourages the reader to be involved in solving the crime along with the Blyton characters. Readers are drawn through the story by an eagerness to solve the crime or find out what happens. In *The Secret Seven Mystery* we are introduced to the detectives before the story starts as their pictures are on the first page. As we begin to read the narrative, Peter and Janet's father identifies the mystery for the Secret Seven to solve:

> His father put down the paper and smiled. 'Do the Secret Seven want to make themselves really useful?' he asked. 'Because I've just read something in my paper that may be right up their street!'
> 'Oh, Dad – What?' cried Peter, and Janet put down her egg-spoon and looked at

him expectantly.

'It's about a girl who's run away from home,' said their father, looking at his paper. 'She stole some money from the desk of her form mistress, but when the police went to see her aunt about it, she ran away.'

The Secret Seven solve the mystery as usual and find that the missing girl is disguised as Tom the stable boy, who has been trying to put them off the scent,

Tears began to fall down the girl's face. 'Yes – I am Elizabeth Sonning! Oh, is it true that Lucy said she took the money? I thought she had – but I wasn't sure. Nobody will think me a thief anymore?'

Throughout the Famous Five and Secret Seven books the reader knows that everything will be resolved in the end, the smugglers will be found out or the treasure discovered. There is a sense of anticipation throughout. The sense of adventure and mystery is balanced by the reassurance of the familiar; as Cullingford states (1979); 'security always has the edge over excitement in Enid Blyton.' In a typical scene the Famous Five explore a tunnel within a cave but they do not go too far until they find the steps or a light. The young reader is not too frightened by the suspense. Readers are taken out of their humdrum world for a while but there is always a return to security at the end.

Blyton matches the reader against the characters. Sarland (1983) argues that children of this age are eager to investigate and find out about the world, and in the Blyton novels the readers are set problems to solve and crimes to investigate, along with the Famous Five, as Enid Blyton leaves questions unanswered for both the characters and the readers.

Adults and Children Apart

A further attraction for the young reader is the fact that the adults and children are seen as separate species, almost in different worlds. Often the parents are in a different place, on holiday or in hospital. In *Five are Together Again* the children are given their freedom because:

'You see, neither your uncle nor I have had scarlet fever – so we are in quarantine, and mustn't have anyone near us.'

The children in the Blyton books are always allowed a great deal of independence, far more than children are given nowadays or in fact were given then. The ten year olds at Sheringdale Primary School said that they would never have been given permission to take a boat over to Kirrin Island and spend a week there alone. This independence is attractive to the young reader. The narrative allows them to read and dream of independence that they have never experienced. In the same way Blyton makes the children act as young adults. Nicholas Tucker (1975) argues that children practise at being adults through play, and reading is a sort of internalized play. As Fry (1985) observes:

> In these books, play temporarily becomes adventure, and the world becomes a place of incident, clues and suspects. It is also a place where children have status, where their interpretation of events holds sway, and where their actions have the power to straighten crookedness and end unhappiness. (p. 54)

The children in both series are in a gang, and many children dream of being a gang member. Membership of the group is very important, secrecy and initiation are paramount. It is the cultural order from the child's perspective. The gangs meet in secret places, they have passwords and they have their own rules which must be obeyed:

> Bang! Somebody knocked at the door.
> 'Password, please,' called Peter. He never unlocked the door until the the person outside said the password.

The characters in the series are easy to understand: they are either good or bad. Tucker (1975) notes that there are no characters in the Blyton books as complex as Long John Silver, who is much nearer to real life, in being both good and bad. Perhaps children at this stage in their reading do not want to think about characters who are not straightforward, preferring to know where they stand at first glance.

Style

Within Enid Blyton books the vocabulary is simple and a limited number of words is used. Words that Blyton thought the readers would find difficult she explained within the text. Such words as 'lovely', 'nice', 'dear', 'little' and 'cosy' fill her pages. There is little use of simile or metaphor. She also uses words which children can relate to, even today, because of the way they sound, such words as 'golly' and 'gosh.' The simpleness of this vocabulary is attractive to the inexperienced reader.

A further aspect of the Blyton style is her use of dialogue in preference to description. Much of the story comes to the reader through voices. Inexperienced readers would feel happier reading about concrete rather than abstract events. It is easier for them to read about the action through a one track narrative line than reading passages of description and people's thoughts.

The Influence

Once young readers have gone past their Blyton stage it is important they move on to other more demanding texts and are able to reflect objectively on the series that have supported them through this particular stage of their reading development. The majority of children at Sheringdale had gone on to reading a variety of other authors. I was interested to see if the children could discuss the Blyton books in terms of racism and sexism and also whether they were aware of the formulae that the books had been written to. As the children were no longer involved in the Secret Seven and the Famous Five they were able to discuss the books without feeling threatened. The children were very perceptive about the Blyton writing and the various characters within the books. They pointed out that Anne in the *Famous Five* often was not involved in the adventure but acted the stereotypical girl character. As Timmy aged ten said:

> Enid Blyton was sexist because the girls had to do all the cooking and the boys would have all the adventures.

Blyton was racist not so much because black characters are missing from the novels, understandable at that date, as in her portrayal of circus people, Travellers and foreigners as either the villains or as stupid within the stories.

I encouraged the children to dissect the books and they were able to see quite clearly the formula that she wrote to and why it had appealed to them as readers. As one child remarked:

> I like books in series like the Famous Five, the Secret Seven and Swallows and Amazons. You know they'll be about the same children.

Alex aged ten said he had read a lot of the Secret Seven and although they were quite good, after a while they became boring and too repetitive.

I worked with twelve children in two groups of six and asked them to write a Blyton adventure in pairs, putting themselves as the characters and using the same style and format. All agreed eagerly. The children wrote five stories about the Super Six and the Sensational Six. In each group of six they discussed the characters, the plot and the settings to make sure that there was uniformity within the stories. The stories were given Blyton type titles: A First Mystery; Smugglers at Bay Island; The Super Six and The Mystery Jewels; Super Six and the Treasure Hunt; The Super Six at Aunt Brenda's.

All the stories used a great deal of dialogue; the child characters got into wonderful scrapes when they were away from their parents either staying with an aunt, a grandmother or being allowed to go off alone to a deserted island. Their adventures involved circus people, smugglers, diamonds and lost money. Secret notes were found and codes deciphered, all fitting in well with the Blyton style of writing. The children in fact found the style and formula extremely easy to reproduce and throughout the whole process discussions occurred about the mechanics of the writing.

The stories were written as if in a series. Below is an extract from *The Super Six at Aunt Brenda's*:

> The secret door led to a dark smelly tunnel. They wandered in. Marlon was in front because he was the bravest. Soon they came to a small door made of wood. Marlon opened it and saw Alex tied up in the corner of a small room.
> 'Are you alright Alex?' said Helen.
> 'I'm tied up, would I be alright?' Alex asked.
> 'Yes you will,' said Sophy.
> Marlon saw two shadows and he told the others.
> 'What can we do?' asked Shelly.
> 'I've an idea,' said Lisa. 'We'll leave Shelly here for bait and when they capture her we'll capture them!'
> 'But what can we capture them with?' Helen said.
> 'I think I can see an old fishing net behind Alex,' said Marlon.

Within this short extract we can see some of the characters' personalities, with the aid of the narrator. We are told that Marlon is the bravest; he is also the one who solves the problem of capturing the men who have tied up Alex. Although the children are in the dark tunnel, with shadows in the background, the writers have not made the situation threatening, thus giving the piece a similar feel to a Blyton story, exciting without being too frightening. The children go on to capture the two men who are 'big time smugglers' as the baddies often are in Blyton adventures. After the Police Sergeant has been called and taken the two men away, the children all go to Aunt Brenda's house for high tea.

> 'That was the best tea I have ever had in my whole life!'
> 'Yes' exclaimed Helen. 'It was the perfect ending to the perfect story!'

The five stories were finally published together with illustrations of all the characters, a note to say that they were written in the style of Enid Blyton, and a short biography of Enid Blyton on the back cover. At the publishing party everyone drank ginger beer!

Chapter Eight

Children's Books and the Emotions

Nicola Humble

The book that induces strong emotion is a familiar literary phenomenon: like Jo March in her attic, eating apples and crying over *The Heir of Rad-clyffe,* we have all enjoyed a book that made us weep. Such emotions are not the subject of this essay. My concern is not with books that elicit particular emotional responses from their readers, but with books that tap into possibly troubling emotional reactions already being experienced by a child.

I had intended to call this essay 'Children's Literature and Difficult Emotions', but I began to wonder about the word 'difficult'. Difficult for whom? For the child experiencing it, or for the adult irritated, bored, embarrassed or concerned about the emotion and its expression? Very often, those emotions found most problematic by the parent or teacher are the least traumatic for the child. The pleasure a child gets from contemplating bodily functions, for example, is 'difficult' only for the adults who see it as resulting in inappropriate behaviour. Conversely, fears and anxieties that seem trivial and transitory from an adult's perspective can consume a child's imagination. This issue is more than a simple matter of differing perspectives. Jacqueline Rose (1984) has suggested that children's literature is primarily 'about' adult preconceptions of children and childhood, and has been used historically as an effective means of moulding children to fit these preconceptions. If we accept her point, we need to consider carefully our intentions when we use books to 'deal with' the emotions of children. We need, for instance, to remember that while emotion itself may be a difficult thing in the controlled world of the adult, for a child it is emotional rather than intellectual responses that are the predominant means of coming to terms with the environment.

For the very young child, it has been widely argued, the flux of power-ful emotions, rages and desires all-consuming in their intensity, is the very stuff of experience. Part of the process of socialization undergone by the child involves learning how to identify, name and control these emotions, and – much more difficult – to become aware of the emotions experienced by others. In this, books can help (as exemplified in practical terms in Mary Walsh's description of children's reactions, Chapter 14).

We can usefully divide the emotions into two types. Firstly, there are those deeply embedded infantile desires and fears that are the concern of psychoanalytic theory. It has been argued by many theorists, following Freud, that literature, like dreams, provides a 'safe' arena for the experi-encing of such unconscious impulses. Nicholas Tucker (1981) argues that children's literature is particularly effective in allowing taboo feelings or fantasies to be acted out. Emotions that might fall into this category are profound and ambivalent responses to parents or parental figures, the simultaneous fear of and desire for a parent's death, for instance. While acknowledging the importance of this category of emotion, I feel that it is a phenomenon that has been adequately discussed in works such as Tucker's, and in Bettelheim's books on fairy tales, and for this reason I propose to concentrate instead on my second category of emotions: those that are fully conscious. These emotions tend to be associated with specific negative, or potentially frightening or disturbing events, such as the death of a close family member, illness, physical changes, starting school, bully-ing, or abuse. Clearly the two categories are in some way linked – the death of a parent could result in uncontrollable feelings of guilt in a child who had subconsciously desired such an event – however, the conscious, event-associated emotions are easier to identify and to address in literature.

In focusing primarily on conscious, nameable emotional responses, I am considering ways in which children's books might enable children to identify their own emotions. Other potential functions of literature that addresses emotions might include enabling a controlled acting out of an emotion; providing time and space to think through a problem; providing possible suggestions for action, or a solution to a problem; and indicating to a child that she is not alone in feeling as she does. Books alone cannot be a solution to the problems of children, but they can provide a starting place and a talking point to allow powerful emotions to be discussed.

While handbooks thinly disguised as fiction on coping with your par-ents' divorce or your first menstrual period might appear to be an exclu-sively modern phenomenon, the history of children's literature reveals that in fact, in its early days, its primary purpose was instruction; entertainment came later – the spoonful of sugar to coax the medicinal message on its way. The early tracts warning of dire punishments for disobedient children were gradually replaced in the course of the nineteenth century by stories of fantasy, mystery and adventure, but the instructive vein remained strong, although it was more likely to take the form of implied social and ideological values – as in the codes of Empire strongly extolled in Kipling's *Stalky & Co.* – than direct exhortations to certain forms of behaviour.

In the first half of the twentieth century children's books reflected the dominant social codes of emotional reticence. The tough avoidance of emotion, particularly sentimentality, is most clearly signalled by the omission of death as a subject in books for children. E. B. White's *Charlotte's Web* of 1952 is considered notable as the first significant book for virtually fifty years to depict the death of a central character. Its poignant description of the spider Charlotte slipping quietly into death as her thousands of children take to the air is still a model for a sensitive, unfrightening approach to this difficult subject.

In the last few decades many people concerned with children's literature have raised objections to its being viewed as entirely, or even largely, instructive, arguing that its primary function should be to entertain and to establish a love of reading. This debate has been complicated by the issue of the felt need for 'positive images' of women, of minority races, of those with disabilities and of non-standard family groups. In my selection of texts I have tried to include some which respond to this social imperative with both sensitivity and aesthetic integrity.

We can observe two major tendencies in children's literature that deals with problems and the emotions they evoke. Firstly there are those texts designed to do so – 'problem' literature that foregrounds a single issue and attempts to effect a textual solution or resolution. These books are usually social realist in form and assumptions. Secondly, there is the literature that is primarily for entertainment, but secondarily addresses problematic emotions, doing so often through the processes of fantasy, and therefore through a displaced rather than a direct identification.

The first tendency, 'problem literature', has proved consistently unpopular with educationalists and literary critics – and equally popular with children. This popularity is not, in itself, sufficient reason to recommend these books – they may be popular because they are unchallenging, in their use of stereotypical characters, predictable plots and easy excitement. It does suggest, however, that they might merit closer examination.

Judy Blume, the major exponent of the genre, writes for ages from six to sixteen. Her subjects include scoliosis – curvature of the spine (*Deenie*), parental divorce (*Just as Long as We're Together*, *It's not the End of the World*), obesity *(Blubber)*, puberty *(Are You There God? It's Me, Mar-*

garet), teenage sex *(Forever)* and parental death *(Tiger Eyes)*. Her narratives are usually first person accounts in the voices of adolescent girls. The texts are upfront in their focus on a specific issue, but rarely crassly simplistic, and the earnest intentions behind them are undoubted. *Deenie* contains a wealth of careful research about scoliosis and its treatment, and doesn't gloss over the discomfort or the acute social embarrassment of wearing a corrective back brace. This book has, to my knowledge, proved helpful to at least one girl with this condition, but perhaps more for its practical information and airing of the subject than as a result of any cathartic effect produced by its literary processes. Blume's texts very rarely get beneath the surface of their subjects: the emotions described are conventional, and seen only externally.

Much of the limitation of Blume's well-intentioned books lies in the narrative voice she adopts. Her protagonists are indistinguishable one from another, and behind each lurks the kindly authorial presence, careful not to press home her moral too violently, but ensuring that it is received loud and clear. This is Stephanie, from *Just as Long as We're Together,* observing her popular friend:

> The funny thing is, Alison doesn't even try to be popular. It's just that everyone wants to be her friend . . . Alison knows how to be popular without being snobby . . . You can learn a lot by watching a popular person in action. (pp. 64–5)

This is precisely the tone of *Jackie* or *My Guy* giving advice on social skills. There is certainly no gap between Stephanie's perception and the authorial presence. Alison is as perfect as she appears, popularity is a worthy and attainable goal if only you work hard at it.

Blume's fictions are above all conventional, extolling the virtues of the family and the well-adjusted, socially integrated adolescent. Anne Fine's novels, in contrast, present stroppy, individualistic characters, often out of sorts with their families and the world. Contemporary social issues such as divorce, old age and gender conditioning form the subject matter of most of her novels, although the approach to these subjects tends to be sufficiently oblique to place her fictions in the second of my two categories. In *Goggle-Eyes*, however, Fine produces the single focus on problem-emotion-solution characteristic of the 'problem novel' tendency, but with a narrative technique that lifts the novel out of the Judy Blume class of bland social realism. The problem of establishing a voice in which to offer solutions is solved by the device of having one child advise another. The novel honestly foregrounds, rather than attempting to disguise, its own status as advice, and gives the advising role to a character rather than to the text itself. The narrator, Kitty, is sent by her form teacher to sit in the lost property cupboard and comfort the distraught Helly. She is selected for this 'delicate mission' because she and Helly share the same problem – prospective stepfathers whom they dislike and resent. In recounting the story of her campaign of attrition against the usurping Goggle-Eyes, and her gradual realisation of his redeeming qualities, Kitty succeeds in evoking Helly's sympathy for Goggle-Eyes and, by extension, for her own villain.

Kitty's success, in what is a neat comment on the power of fiction to approach problems and emotions, is not simply a result of her having shared Helly's experience. She is successful because she is a story-teller, skilled at transforming her experience into fiction, and thereby gaining power over it:

> 'What happened?' she asked. 'Don't stop, Go on. Tell me what happened.'
> That's how I like my listeners – craving for more. Mrs Lupey isn't Head of English in our school for nothing . . . She begged for the last instalment of my serial *Tales From a Once Happy Home*. Oh, yes. Mrs Lupey knew one thing when she passed over Liz for Mission Helen, and sent me out instead. When it comes to a story, I just tell 'em better. (p. 46)

While Blume's world is peopled with conforming children and adults either stereotypically flawed – drunken, divorcing, absent – or blandly caring, Fine's characters are sharply distinguished and finely drawn. Kitty's mother, volatile, happily flirting and passionately rowing with her new partner, getting herself arrested on anti-nuclear demonstrations, is a believably complex character, and her daughter's frustration at her vacillating moods is convincing. In *Goggle-Eyes*, Fine achieves a delicate blend of problem solving with storytelling, never once sacrificing interesting characters and responses to the requirements of social realism or moralising.

The above fictions address themselves to the concerns of older children and adolescents. The fears and emotions of younger children are somewhat different – less articulated, less social, more concerned with the sensations of the present than with anticipating the future. This difference is clearly represented in the various emotions and problems focused on by 'problem' literature. For the older age group (over tens), as noted, parental divorce and the social and physical adjustments of adolescence are most covered. Seven to ten year olds, perhaps less well served with 'problem' literature than other age groups, are offered friendship and sibling rivalry. For the under sevens the major topic seems to be fear of the dark, closely followed by starting school and the birth of a new sibling. Where picture books are concerned, the divergence between the overt and the displaced approaches to the problems is less marked. The particular form of the picture book, with its relatively sparse text, and freely interpretable images imports imaginative elements into even the most crassly instructive story.

This is most clearly demonstrable if we consider those texts concerned with the fear of the dark. Precisely because this fear is compounded of imagination, books need to depict the images of fear, the monsters and witches in the dark corners of the room, in order to dispel them. Where texts differ is in their approach to these fearful creatures. We can establish a continuum of texts on a spectrum from commonsense realism to out and out fantasy. Analise Taylor's *Lights Off, Lights On* conjures up shadowy monsters on each page, only to dispel them by revealing their true identity when the lights are on:

> There's a stranger behind the door
> I've seen him standing there before
> So tall and dark as he looks down
> Silly me! It's my dressing gown!

Nigel Snell, in *Danny is Afraid of the Dark* also conjures up monsters – a bat and a goblin – that Mother reveals as just a dressing-gown and a pile of clothes. The reader, however, can see the blue goblin hiding under Danny's bed, and on the last page we are shown him and the bat going 'sadly away because they knew Danny didn't believe in them any more'. The objects of the child's imagination are not, as in Taylor's story, dismissed as fanciful, but rather vanquished by his refusal to believe. This more subtle exorcism is marred, however, by the scrappy quality of the illustrations in Snell's book.

A more recent picture book which plays enjoyably with the child's fear is Ruth Brown's *A Dark, Dark Tale*. Its lovely, spooky, elegant illustrations start with a dark, dark house in a wood and move through its gothic interior in closer and closer focus to reveal a box in a dark, dark, corner. The final denouement – 'And in the box there was A MOUSE!' – reveals a miniature domestic setting of a tiny mouse in an old fashioned bedroom, the picture illuminated by the golden light from his candle. The suspense is beautifully maintained, and the fear ingeniously controlled: in the end it is the mouse who looks fearfully up at us as we disturb his rest.

Animal characters are often employed very effectively in picture books to facilitate a dual process of distancing and re-identification. The animal is initially attractive because it is *not* another child, but the child reader is delighted to find similarities between its life and her own. Franz Brandenberg and James Stevenson's *Otto is Different* employs an octopus protagonist to approach the problem of 'difference' – whether of race, appearance, or physical ability. It is powerful treatment, because Otto's difference is actually a potential advantage, once he looks at it in the right way: the eight arms which he has refused to use because he wants to be more like his friends:

'Use your arms, Otto!' said Mother.

'I do', said Otto.

'But not all of them,' said Mother.

'Oh, why do we have to be different!' said Otto. 'Why can't we be like everyone else!'

Once he discovers the advantages of eight arms he becomes happy, successful and popular. The energetic watercolours of the octopus family contribute to the upbeat feel of the story. The combination of the fantastic or make-believe with the everyday, here represented by an octopus playing hockey and being hugged by his mother, is one that is employed in various forms by many very accomplished children's writers. Fantasy can be very effective, both in approaching and in resolving emotional problems, because its processes of making the strange familiar and the familiar strange require an emotional identification to occur prior to a rational one. The reader, caught up in adventure or excitement, will unconsciously make the different world presented accessible to his or her own experience by looking for emotional parallels, and developing an empathy for the characters despite the differences in their situations. This process sidesteps the irritated resistance with which many readers – child or adult – respond to a book that is obviously seeking to 'preach' to them.

The clearest example of this sort of writing is that of Diana Wynne Jones, in my view the best children's writer of the last decade. Her stories of time travel, of parallel worlds where magic is everyday, and of myths strangely transformed, are peopled by recognisable children, who often feel themselves outsiders, less talented than their peers. Yet these are not merely tales of rebellious disaffection; they are also parables of otherness, and of the need to realize individual potential. *Witch Week* applies the child's feeling of inferiority to the familiar day-to-day world of a school, a strict mixed state boarding school called Larwood House. Class 2Y's journal writing is interrupted one morning when their form teacher receives an anonymous note claiming that 'Someone in this class is a witch'. The consternation this causes among staff and pupils is explained as we begin to understand that the story is set not in our own society, but in a parallel world, where witches are still burned at the stake. Apart from this anomaly, the setting is entirely conventional, and the details of school rivalries and occupations are precisely captured. This is Nan Pilgrim, one of the disaffected central characters, describing the class hierarchy in her journal:

I do not know if 2Y is average or not, but this is how they are. They are divided into girls and boys with an invisible line down the middle of the room and people only cross that line when teachers make them. Girls are divided into real girls (Theresa Mullett) and imitations (Estelle Green). And me. Boys are divided into real boys (Simon Silverston), brutes (Daniel Smith) and unreal boys (Nirupam Singh). And Charles Morgan. and Brian Wentworth. What makes you a real girl or boy is that no one laughs at you. If you are imitation or unreal, the rules give you a right to exist provided you do what the real ones or brutes say. What makes you into me or Charles Morgan is that the rules allow all the girls to be better than me and all the boys to be better than Charles Morgan. They are allowed to cross the invisible line to prove this. Everyone is allowed to cross the invisible line to be nasty to Brian Wentworth. (pp. 37–8)

As a description of the finely graduated jungle politics of a classroom, this is hard to beat. The novel ingeniously combines the forms and themes of science fiction, fantasy, the mystery, and the school story to produce some telling lessons about the mechanisms of power and prejudice, and the motivations and feelings of bullies and their victims. Wynne Jones has a light touch with the paradoxes of science fiction, and, like all the best fantasy, her stories are intellectually as well as emotionally nourishing, the possibilities they create lingering in the mind long after they are read.

All of the fictions I have discussed have, I contend, some part to play in speaking to the emotions of the child reader, but this is not an exact science. Some texts will reach deeper than others, and none will prove effective or meaningful for every child. Perhaps the most valuable thing literature can offer children is a sense of emotional empathy for, and generosity towards, other people and their experiences, developing out of an intense identification with the lives of fictional characters, and a sense of places, people and feelings beyond the here and now. As Kitty, narrator of *Goggle-Eyes*, informs us:

> Living your life is a long and doggy business, says Mrs Lupey. And stories and books help. Some help you with the living itself. Some help you just take a break. The best do both at the same time. (p. 139)

Books referred to and suggestions for further reading

FOR CHILDREN UNDER TEN

Ahlberg, Janet & Allan (1988) *Starting School*. London: Viking Kestrel

Blume, Judy (1982) *Superfudge*. London: Piccolo. A tale of a frustrating younger brother.

Brandenberg, Franz & Stevenson, James. (9185) *Otto is Different*. London: Julia Macrae

Brown, Ruth (1981) *A Dark, Dark Tale*. London: Random Century Children's Books

Fine, Anne (1990) *Bill's New Frock*. London: Mammoth. A highly effective humorous look at the effect of gender conditioning on children.

Harper, Anita & Roche, Christine (1979) *How We Feel*. Harmondsworth: Penguin. A jaunty survey of all sorts of feelings, for children of about four or five.

Hoffman, Mary & Binch, Caroline (1982) *Amazing Grace*. London: Frances Lincoln. Charming central character offers positive images of race and gender and a lesson about perseverance for timid children.

Keats, Ezra Jack (1988) *Peter's Chair*. London: Bodley Head. Adjusting to a new sibling.

Keller, Holly (1991) *The New Boy*. London: Julia MacRae. Assorted rodents as new infants.

Sendak, Maurice (1975) *Where the Wild Things Are*. London: Bodley Head. The classic story of monsters of the imagination and a child's gaining power over them.

Snell, Nigel (1982) *Danny is Afraid of the Dark*. London: Hamish Hamilton

Taylor, Analise (1977) *Lights Off, Lights On*. Oxford: Oxford University Press

White, E.B. (1952) *Charlotte's Web*. London: Hamish Hamilton

For Children over Ten

Blume, Judy (1988) *Are You There God? It's Me, Margaret*.
(1988) *Deenie*.
(1986) *Forever*.
(1988) *Just as Long as We're Together, It's Not the End of the World*
(1988) *Tiger Eyes*

All London: Pan

Cresswell, Helen (1982) *Dear Shrink*. London: Faber. An upbeat adventure, which is also an account of foster homes and care institutions.

Fine, Anne (1990) *Goggle Eyes*. Harmondsworth: Penguin

Gardam, Jane (1976) *Bilgewater*. London: Hamish Hamilton. The classic example of a text focusing on the outsider's experience of adolescence: tough, witty and poignant.

Greene, Bette (1979) *Philip Hall likes me, I reckon, maybe*. Harmondsworth: Penguin. Adolescent rivalry and egoism. All the characters are black, but this is simply the prevailing background rather than a problem, and they provide strong role models.

Sacks, Marilyn (1984) *The Fat Girl*. London: Corgi

Salinger, J.D. (1951) *The Catcher in the Rye*. Harmondsworth: Penguin. Still among the most compelling accounts of adolescence.

Wynne Jones, Diana (1977) *The Ogre Downstairs*. Harmondsworth: Penguin. A fresh look at the problems of step-families.

Wynne Jones, Diana (1989) *Power of Three*. London: Macmillan. A powerful fantasy, also a parable about race and environmental issues.

Wynne Jones, Diana (1979) *Witch Week*. London: Macmillan

Chapter Nine

Finding the Right Book for a Reader

Philippa Hunt

I thought it would be so easy. I had done everything correctly. I had even gone on *Newsnight* at the start of yet another reading standards storm and confidently predicted that, because I had done all the right things, my son would be a *proper* reader, an independent reader, a reader who would read because he wanted to not because he had learnt how to decode print in a meaningless way. He was seven then and could read; he was able to pick up quite difficult books when asked and confidently and fluently decode the words. If the National reading tests for seven year olds had been around, he would have reached the above average level of 3, maybe even level 4, and all this had been achieved without a dreary reading scheme or phonic building blocks. His Primary school enthusiastically embraced 'The Real Books' method for teaching reading. This did not mean he was left amongst a pile of books to learn to read by some process rather like osmosis; rather he could choose books he wanted to read and his choice and progress were carefully monitored. He brought home the books as part of a PACT (Parents, Children and Teachers) scheme so we felt involved in his development.

So why did I feel something had gone wrong when he reached the age of eight? I had imagined that a good reader, one that had been exposed to interesting books all his life and had always loved hearing stories, would have no problem moving from listening to stories to turning the pages himself. But it didn't happen. He still loved to curl up on his bed and become absorbed in other worlds but I could not persuade him to take himself to these other places. Was it laziness? I felt it was. Children today do have their pleasures served up more effortlessly: hours of enjoyment can be had with the flick of a switch. However I am now convinced that more importantly it was a question of finding the right book. Thomas became a reader the day he discovered Lynne Reid Banks's *The Indian in The Cupboard*, a book recommended to me by a Primary school teacher friend. I started it for him, reading the first few pages, and he was hooked. The book was finished in two days and he was asking for more. Why did this book succeed where so many others had failed? One reason may have been the combination of a fairly sophisticated storyline with uncomplicated vocabulary and substantial dialogue.

I read it myself later and became absorbed in the idea of a plastic toy Indian coming alive in a small cupboard. The fascination of small things coping in the 'human beings' world obviously has lasting appeal; hence the continuing popularity of Mary Norton's *The Borrowers*. I now realise that before *The Indian in The Cupboard*, I may well have offered Thomas stories of which he found either the content too babyish or the text too difficult.

Having got Thomas reading at last, I could not sit back and enjoy the comforting sight of a child happily employed with a book. There are, I know, some children who need no encouragement: put them in a library and they feel spoilt for choice. These readers think nothing of putting down the latest Betsy Byars and picking up Frances Hodgson Burnett's *The Secret Garden*. There are however many more who need continual guidance and encouragement and it is adults who mainly have to provide this if reading is to become and remain a chosen activity. Other children who can read but choose not to might also find *The Indian in The Cupboard* irresistible but their parents or teachers will, like me, have to seek ways to keep the reading habit going. My experience as a parent, although more personal, has many similarities to my concerns as a secondary English teacher. Over a hundred pupils would spend approximately two and a half hours a week in my classroom and in that time, amongst all the other pressing demands on an English teacher, I wanted to encourage or sustain the reading habit in as many of them as possible.

Finding out as much as possible about an individual's reading profile was one of my top priorities when taking over a class. I used a variety of strategies including personal interviews during library lessons, pupils' written accounts of their reading interests and records passed on from former teachers. The National Curriculum for English, introduced since I ceased being a classroom teacher, recommends that pupils make personal reading lists as evidence of their reading progress. I used a box file kept on my desk for this purpose. Each pupil had a card which was colour-coded to indicate which year of the secondary school they were in. When they read a book, they added the title and author to their card plus the date of completion. Pupils enjoyed the ritual and felt some pride in the list expanding. For me it was a quick and efficient way of keeping an eye on what individuals were reading. Non-readers were easily spotted while the readers limited by author or genre could be identified and guided by another box file. In this other box, I kept cards listing books arranged in categories such as themes, authors and follow-up suggestions for class readers. A pupil who loved romantic fiction but had read little more than Sweet Valley High books could find other suggested titles with a short description as guidance. I had read some of the books myself but I used magazines like *Books for Keeps* and *The English Magazine* to keep me abreast of latest publications.

Children's librarians can also be an invaluable source of information for teachers, parents and children. Ceri Worman, until recently the Senior Children's Librarian for Wandsworth, knows how hard it is for some readers to find the right book when faced with shelves of possibilities. She feels that asking what previous titles have been read and enjoyed is the best way to start. Children remember titles rather than authors although very popular writers such as Judy Blume might well be mentioned and will be helpful for sorting out other authors or titles. If titles cannot be recalled, she asks about genres: Do you like science fiction? Are you interested in sport? Do you enjoy being scared? Questions like these help when trying to find out what will appeal to the potential reader but unless you have some knowledge of what can be offered, this knowledge is worthless. Librarians like Ceri are in a better position to keep abreast of what is being published because they receive copies of the new books on the market but they, like English teachers, have to get to know the range of what is on offer and to what sort of readers certain books might appeal. Anyone interested in developing the reading interests of children must read as much children's literature as they can and then store this knowledge somehow so that when a poor but keen reader asks for an exciting mystery story, s/he is not only offered a Sherlock Holmes book.

The box file on my desk was my way of having some information on books at my fingertips. I found another use for a box file at home. I gave Thomas his own red file so that he could build up a history of his reading. Every book read has been recorded individually on a card and filed under the author's name. The date of completion and brief comments have been added and now, two years later, there is a satisfying bulk of cards recording a young person's reading history. It is interesting that none of the named books on the latest reading list from the National Curriculum Council have a card although he does know all of these books. He has come to these books through other means: for example, he has seen a play version of Lewis Carroll's *Alice's Adventures in Wonderland*, I read him A.A. Milne's *Winnie the Pooh* and he listened to Kipling's *The Jungle Book* on a tape. Without these aids I doubt Thomas would know these books at all and I support the idea that teachers should search for ways to help all pupils know these classics. What Thomas has recorded on his cards is a genuine list which might not exist at all if I did not keep searching for books that work for him.

Finding the right book continues to be a struggle. Friends' recommendations are worth pursuing but cannot be guaranteed: Ian Serraillier's *The Silver Sword* was an immediate hit while a Willard Price was abandoned after the opening chapter. A trustworthy critic is worth finding. In a summer edition of *The Times Educational Supplement* I discovered a short article by Victor Watson called 'Quests for all Ages.' He made some suggestions for children's holiday reading from recently published fiction. I was desperate for some ideas for our imminent holiday and rushed round finding copies of about five of the books described. Without exception, they were enthusiastically devoured, each one proclaimed better than the last. Such continuous success had not been achieved before and I shall now leap to acquire any book which has Victor Watson's stamp of approval.

Of course we want our children and our pupils to learn to make choices on their own. The more we read the easier it is to do this. We learn to trust authors, read the back page of the cover and search in the right parts of libraries and bookshops. But even as a keen adult reader, I depend on friends' recommendations for many of the books I read. Why should it be any different for young people? They just need to learn who to ask.

Parents and teachers who want their children to discover the power of the page must not expect it to come easy. Many adults who talk fondly of their childhood when they flew with Peter Pan, sailed ships in rivers and discovered islands with pirates forget that children today can do all these things and more by renting the latest video. We may resent and regret this but we cannot ignore it. We just have to work harder to find the space for reading and then to fill that space with the right book.

Books referred to in this chapter

Banks, Lynne Reid (1981) *The Indian in The Cupboard.* London: Collins
Burnett, Frances Hodgson (1976) *The Secret Garden.* London: Heinemann
Carroll, Lewis (1976) *Alice's Adventures in Wonderland.* Harmondsworth: Penguin
Kipling, Rudyard (1967) *The Jungle Book.* London: Pan
Milne, A.A. (1965) *Winnie The Pooh.* London: Methuen
Norton, Mary (1958) *The Borrowers.* Harmondsworth: Puffin
Serraillier, Ian (1960) *The Silver Sword.* Harmondsworth: Penguin

Chapter Ten

Moving On: Becoming a Mature Reader

Jacquie Nunn

'If it's a good writer, you feel like you're there. I much prefer reading.'
'I usually wait for the video to come out.'

Books can tell you lots more about people's feelings and what they think.'
'Of course you need to learn to read . . . you'll have to read the gas bill!'

These contrasting opinions, from thirteen and fourteen year old readers, sum up a dilemma for many concerned with children's reading. We may not be beguiled by the siren voices of those who insist current teaching methods have resulted in a general decline in reading ability. We can even draw comfort from the evidence of the Publishers Association which shows that over a ten year period the British read more books than any European nation with the exception of Germany (Publishers Association Trade Year Book 1992). And yet there remains the awareness that while many young adults leave school with a love of books, many others have an entirely functional attitude to reading. Recent concern about reading standards has focused attention on the ability of the individual child to decode print while diverting attention from the equally interesting question as to what use a young reader makes of the skill once acquired.

There have, of course, been descriptions of the process of acquiring literacy and of the subsequent development of the individual as a reader. The *Primary Language Record* (Barrs et al. 1988) focuses on the developing ability to cope with a range of fiction and non-fiction texts in terms of a continuum from inexperienced to experienced reader, achieved at or about Primary/Secondary transfer stage. The Attainment Targets of the National Curriculum in English (DES 1990) embody a hierarchy of reading skills moving from the infant's understanding that print carries meaning, to the ability to analyse style and purpose in the above average young adult. (DES 1990). There are fewer accounts of reading development beyond formal schooling. Appleyard (1990) characterises the process in terms of psychological development: the player reader of the early years becomes the reader heroine of childhood, who evolves into the reflective reader thinker of adolescence, the reader interpreter of young adulthood and the pragmatic reader of middle-age.

Any such developmental model of reading shifts our attention from the issue of acquisition of basic literacy. It will also make us examine which practices at home and in the classroom will help children along this continuum. We need to consider which kinds of texts will support development and the reasons why large numbers of competent de-coders of print never reach the point where they would happily describe themselves as 'readers'.

The Reader

This raises the question of how we might identify the reading habits which are characteristic of mature readers. A competent adult reader might well begin the analysis on the bedside table. That might contain a wide range of material: professional or academic journals, non-fiction books relevant to leisure interests, magazines, 'serious' literature, alongside the latest blockbuster fiction. Such a range of texts demands a matching range of reading styles including skimming, scanning, reflective rereading. Being a 'good' reader has less to do with reading 'good' texts than with exercising a range of reading skills.

As part of the small-scale research project into reading carried out in London primary and secondary schools, I interviewed groups of nine and ten year olds about their reading and the evidence confirmed that some children acquire these flexible and critical reading habits early on. These young readers described dipping into reference books for information to support topic work, close reading of fiction by favourite authors and skimming through texts already familiar to them. These children were aware of the dates when books were published; when for example, they looked at an atlas which referred to East and West Germany, they were critical of books containing obsolete information. They were also able to name preferred authors and genres of reading and to look out for books that matched their developing interests.

Other children were apparently dependent on one style of reading, beginning at the beginning and working doggedly through the text whatever the purpose. This group were much more reliant upon the suggestions of their teacher for their private reading, less likely to buy books for themselves and less frequent visitors to the local library.

The first group are already showing in their reading some of the skills typical of good readers: they re-evaluate; they anticipate; they enter into a dialogue with the author; they establish a relationship with certain authors; they adapt their reading technique for specific purposes; they question the text.

Not all young readers move on from this confident base to become discriminating, independent readers as adults. One key factor is gender. This is borne out by the large scale research studies carried out by the NFER (Gorman 1987). While there is much overlap in the early years between the reading habits of boys and girls, by the teens girls typically choose books with romance, relationships and human issues as their themes while boys frequently resort to non-fiction books to support hobbies and interests. Boys in my study frequently described reading as a passive activity and rated it lower than more active pursuits. While 90 per cent of nine year old girls described themselves as 'readers' fewer than 50 per cent of the boys did, numbers which fell to 50 per cent and 37 per cent respectively at the age of thirteen.

Once basic literacy has been acquired then, the teacher has a key role in developing the child's self-awareness as a reader, building on early reading skills through provision of the widest possible range of reading experience. In the Primary phase the teacher is able to monitor this development from a cross-curricular perspective and can acquire an understanding of the child as a reader across a range of genres and for a variety of purposes. After the transition to the Secondary level, evidence shows that much reading takes place in fragmented and spasmodic chunks. (Southgate et al 1981). It may be then that the private reading lesson in English provides the only time for sustained reading. The world of children's books is far wider than the category of fiction and it is a strength of the National Curriculum that English teachers in the secondary classroom are required to include study of non-fiction genres such as travel, biography, diaries and letters. Analysing the different ways in which such texts represent ideas and experience extends the language approaches developed in the Primary phase through topic work.

But before teachers can begin to plan for this kind of development they need more detailed information about individual reading habits and attitudes to books than is to be gained from the National Curriculum levels of attainment. Much useful information can be gained through use of questionnaires for whole year groups or for individual classes, although these need amplifying if possible. Group interviews can be a useful technique and if developed around a loosely structured format they can give the teacher helpful insights into the ways in which young readers perceive books. In my study, one boy who showed little inclination to read in school talked happily about reading aloud to a younger sister. These perceptions of the child as reader make it much more likely that the teacher will be able to plan and monitor future development. In this instance the class teacher fostered the child's self esteem and identity as a reader by arranging paired reading with younger children in the school. Conferences with parents are a valuable tactic, although time-consuming and more difficult to organise at Secondary than at Primary level. It is, however, possible to make reading a specific topic of discussion at parents' meetings. Reading logs and journals, structured or unstructured, can be invaluable in monitoring individual development. They will be incomplete however unless they include out-of-school reading as well as that done in the classroom: most of the children I surveyed reported that they read more at home than in school.

A great deal of useful information can be gathered quickly following the simple method suggested by Andrew Stibbs (1978). The teacher watches the class as they read the same text, to see who is absorbed, who is distracted, who reads slowly and who skims along. The reading lesson in school also provides an opportunity for the teacher to model for students some of the ways in which mature readers approach texts. This could include tactics for choosing books such as the use of bookjackets, blurbs, skimming the opening pages, making predictions and talking about individual authors. It is especially important to introduce genres that may be unfamiliar to students, including adult contemporary fiction. One fifteen year old boy who came across Luke Reinhardt's *The Dice Man* after seeing his teacher reading it during private reading said, 'I didn't know that books could be like that.' For him this surprising discovery bridged the gap between childhood and adult reading.

Contexts for Reading

This kind of reading development can only take place in an environment which allows young readers to share their pleasure in books, to develop preferences and pursue enthusiasms. Unfortunately there are many disadvantages of the classroom as a context for this activity. Reading in the company of thirty others, for a finite period of time and sitting on a hard seat may be sound preparation for computer-reading but it is not the obvious setting for relaxing with a book. Primary classrooms often feature a book corner with cushions and carpet but secondary classrooms rarely do this even when specialist English areas are designated.

Children at both secondary and primary level in my survey said that they preferred to read at home and for many of them it was at bed-time, a habit acquired with the story-time habits of early childhood. Contexts for reading then embody more than the physical environment but include the cultural and social contexts of family and peer group reading. Much research indicates the importance of family orientations to literacy; indeed Wells (1987) suggests that the most significant factor in predicting educational achievement across all subject areas is experience of narrative in early childhood. A striking feature of my study was that keen readers had a clear sense of their parents as readers, volunteering such detailed or even controversial information as:

> 'My mum likes comedy, she reads politics and black writers like Alice Walker and Rosa Guy.'
> 'My mum enjoys story books but my dad reads non-fiction because he has a job to do!'

The literacy habits of the family are the central influence on young readers. As Heath (1983) puts it, families shape the way children learn to make meaning from their environment, and this includes making sense of the world through books. In families rooted in a literate tradition this will include not only taking meaning from books but also learning how to talk about it. But there are endless variations on family orientations to literacy. In my own study there were children who had access to few fiction books at home although parents had invested in encyclopaedias and other reference works. For some, family literacy was associated with learning Arabic as part of Qur'anic education. Another boy reported that his bed-time reading consisted entirely of Bible stories. For all of these young readers, school can provide an alternative 'critical community' where readers may reflect together upon texts not encountered at home.

English teachers, parents and librarians need to be prepared to defend the value of this experience. The essential resources for reading are being threatened. Subject areas are struggling to maintain their allocation of an already crowded timetable. Meanwhile less is being spent on books in real terms and such funds as are available are earmarked for the provision of set texts in large numbers. Another factor constraining young readers at a formative time is the pressure of work for examinations. For many fifteen and sixteen year olds who are on the point of becoming adult readers, the combination of social activities and preparation for examinations leaves little time for sustained private reading. Reading can become associated with other tedious aspects of school work, which is contrary to the perception of reading as a pleasurable and personally rewarding habit which teachers would advocate.

A key factor, then, in the development of young adults into readers is the importance which the school attaches to reading and the way in which it seeks to promote itself as a community of readers. Numerous activities formal and informal can contribute to this. They include:

- Book weeks, combining displays with author visits, performances, publications and parental involvement. Such activities can sometimes be funded by regional arts associations even when school budgets are restricted.
- School bookshops: as many young readers suggest that they find it difficult to find the books they like, they should be consulted on the stock.
- Display of reviews in the school library, wall charts and posters in English classrooms and in the corridor areas. Use of the school newsletter or magazine for reader-reviews of books recently arrived in school.
- Use of databases such as Bookstore (ESM software/for Archimedes) which allows readers to enter reviews using a ready made format and then retrieve their own or other pupils' reviews, searching for favourite author, title or type of book.

All of these are practical ways in which teachers or librarians can develop reading as a public activity and create a shared context for critical reading. Other more subversive aspects of reading should not be ignored. Reading shared with others in the peer group can be a powerful formative influence, beginning in the book corner in the primary classroom and continuing well into the secondary years, while for many adult readers sharing and recommending books with friends is part of the pleasure of reading. Research carried out in Oxfordshire schools (West 1987) showed that in one school where reading was thriving a key identifiable factor was the practice of 'networking', that is groups of readers exchanging books and sharing ideas and responses. Gender issues may be significant here. In one London school where all-boy groups were established to counteract a gender imbalance, teachers observed that boys in single-sex groups shared ideas about books more readily and were more willing to talk about books that dealt with emotions, such as those by Judy Blume, than were the boys in mixed groups. Some intervention may then be appropriate in organising groups for wider reading.

All of these public aspects of reading are important when it comes to establishing a context for reading development, Nevertheless when we talk about the experience of being 'lost in a book' we recognise the unique power of a book to create its own context. And if we are anxious for young readers to share in this experience we need to pay attention to the kinds of books they are reading.

Powerful Books

For young readers to share in the experience of being lost in a text, they need to move beyond the safe and the familiar. Appleyard (1990) suggests that childhood reading is characterised by texts which offer us glimpses of adult worlds, and a limited range of settings. The narrative structure is typically linear; a powerful hero or heroine overcomes a series of dangers and difficulties before the narrative is resolved in a happy conclusion. The centre of interest is action rather than development of the character. It can be argued that this analysis holds true for series like those involving Postman Pat or The Hardy Boys and Nancy Drew as well as the latest from Jackie Collins and that therefore, by that definition, many adult readers remain locked in childhood reading. There is no automatic continuity of development. Clearly there are value judgements implicit in this and it is important to recognise the pleasure principle involved in reading safe and undemanding texts. However, looked at in terms of teenage reading there seems to be a danger. Many of the popular series targeted at the age group: The Point Horror Series, Sweet Valley High or Choose Your Own Adventure emulate the pleasures of the video, the TV soap or the arcade game and inevitably they fall short of the 'real thing'. The power of the page is subordinated to other, non-traditional kinds of 'texts' and the book comes to seem inferior.

Some of the reasons for this may be located in institutional practices, notably the tying in of book promotions with television series and popular films. In the older age range this may account in part for the decline in reading among boys. Many series are targeted principally at girls and boys often complain they have difficulty in finding books that appeal to them. Much of teenage fiction is marketed with an eye on the classroom and the school library. It tends to be focused on social issues and human relationships and is less likely to be characterised by humour which is precisely the quality that many boys look for in stories: witness the enormous popularity of the Asterix books for younger readers.

The teacher's task is to help the young reader to find an appropriate book and then to demonstrate the special pleasures of printed texts. One aspect of this can be what a child in my study described as 'getting inside the person's head'. A key stage in childhood reading is the point where the reader becomes less dependent on illustrations. An analogy with adult reading is the point where a film or TV adaptation of a text can be infuriating or disappointing according to how it correlates with our mental picture of the characters and settings. Although I have considered reading development in terms of shared critical activity, one of the most powerful special pleasures of books remains the sense of a private relationship between reader and writer. That it is a powerful relationship is demonstrated by the fact that the authors young readers admire have in common a strong narrative voice: the subversiveness of Roald Dahl, or the quirky perspective of Betsy Byars are easily recognisable.

In the classroom, explicit work in the context of English or Media studies can help to define for young readers the power of the text and the special ways in which writers convey meaning. If, as Appleyard suggests, a key feature of the transition from childhood reading to mature reader is a shift in focus of interest from action to psychological development of the character, then this process is an important stepping stone. I recently watched an English lesson in which a group of Year 10 students argued energetically about J.G. Ballard's *Empire of the Sun*. Having initially denounced the book as dull because the action did not move swiftly enough, they were intrigued by the motivation of character and the relationship between historical 'truth' and fictionalised narrative. When asked, most of them declared that they would not have chosen the book for themselves as it was apparently an adult book which initially seemed unapproachable. In this case they had been helped through the text and supported in their private reading by small group and whole class study and all of this took place in the context of 'set' reading for examination.

Of course, external agencies, notably examination boards and the National Curriculum Council, have an important influence in defining the range of texts studied. With increasing prescription of the reading curriculum at Key Stages 3 and 4 there is potentially at least a narrowing of the range of books to be read. A conflict is apparent between the statements in the Programmes of Study in the National Curriculum which look for breadth and depth in reading across a range of genres, and the mode of assessment which dictates narrow reading and an emphasis on extracts rather than on complete texts. The consequences of assessment leading the curriculum are dangerous. Appleyard's account of the way in which American college students majoring in Literature respond to texts shows how a rigid assessment framework based on multiple choice questions and simple responses to extracts from texts, limits students' confidence as readers and makes it difficult even for those majoring in Literature to look at aspects of texts other than character and plot.

For many developing readers the power of the text lies not in its place in the canon but in its ability to question and subvert authority, to take risks and to address the difficult and illicit aspects of sexuality or identity, to acknowledge that all endings are not happy. A novel such as Robert Cormier's *The Chocolate War* in which evil characters triumph over the good, proposes a uncomfortable truth about existence with which teenagers can identify. Similar truths can be found in the works of a whole range of authors: Anita Desai, Janni Howker, James Watson, Margaret Mahy, Jan Mark. Such writers break away from the conventional divide of teen reading into romance and human interest for girl readers and horror and science fiction for boys. Above all they offer older readers variety and richness of experience where endings are left unresolved, structure is not linear, the narrative point of view shifts.

Learning to read is a process that begins in infancy and potentially, continues throughout our lives. As Frank Smith puts it (1982) we learn to read by reading. So while there may be no harm in the utilitarian attitudes to reading expressed by the young readers quoted at the beginning of this chapter and while there is undoubtedly pleasure to be had from reading of the safe and the predictable, there are consequences in not extending and developing our reading. It is a myth that we live in a post-literate society. The ability to make sense of the world in which we live is shaped by our ability to read texts of all kinds. But there are personal consequences of our power to make sense of literature. As Bettelheim (1976) puts it, it is through reading that we make contact with our cultural heritage and through literature that we are helped to find meaning in our existence whatever that culture may be. For young readers to make this contact they need access to the widest possible range of books and the support of those whether they be teachers, parents, librarians or friends, who take pleasure from books and are themselves active in the process of learning how to read.

Chapter Eleven

The Individual and Society: Novels for Adolescents

Catherine Sheldon

What is 'teenage fiction', and in what ways is it distinguishable from fiction intended for a younger audience, or even from that intended for adults? The easy answers will not satisfy for long: you have only to watch an eight year old avidly reading Willard Price adventure stories in which nineteen year olds narrowly avoid being devoured by crocodiles, polar bears, or killer whales, or Chalet School adventures where the triplets have to speak in French three times a week, to realize that it is not the age of the central character that determines the target audience.

Some authors gear their work specifically to an adolescent audience by having characters of a suitable age face the problems of their age-group: parental divorce, shortage of money, awakening sexuality. Over the years I must have read dozens of such novels – and can remember almost nothing about any of them. I tend to assume that works of this sort must be of more interest to young people than to adults, so I put them into the school book boxes and let them take their chance. Occasionally a book of this type seems to stand out from the rest, remains in my mind for a longer time and seems interesting enough to pass on to another adult to read. The works of Jean Ure are an example. *The Other Side of the Fence* succeeds in being absorbing to read while dealing sensitively (and surprisingly) with homosexuality, and *One Green Leaf* is about the painful experience of facing the death of an adolescent friend.

However, there are other teenage books that I read for pleasure, that remain in my mind hauntingly, perhaps for years. Novels of Diana Wynne Jones, Margaret Mahy, William Mayne, Ursula le Guin are examples. Such novels can be perceived as relevant both by some young people and some adults. They may rest rather uneasily in the teenage sector of publishers' lists because they take as central characters people embarking on adult life – but Dickens and Charlotte Bronte do the same. In addition, some of their content is too uncompromising for a younger audience, not because of its sexual implications but perhaps because of the harshness of the world it represents or the complexity and depth of the vision it presents. My older daughter, aged eight, loves books by Diana Wynne Jones and has read *Power of Three* and (spurred on by the television serial) *Archer's Goon* half a dozen times each. Other books by the same author, such as *The Home-ward Bounders* or *The Spellcoats*, are not ostensibly aimed at an older audience, but may be better left until the reader is older because they are more uncompromising in the way they lead their characters away from home and safety for ever. There are books that appal, as well as interest and delight: I think of William Mayne's *A Game of Dark* or the wonderfully moving stories in his *All The King's Men*.

Three novels which will perhaps serve to illustrate this are *Aquarius, Divide and Rule* and *The Ennead* by Jan Mark. I find these novels strange, moving and powerfully original. The emotion I am left with after reading them I can only describe as a kind of horrified pity. Each novel is different though each takes as its subject a character just embarking on adult life and becoming aware of the sickening corruption of the adult world and the need to define oneself in relation to it.None of these characters is supported by a peer group: they face the world alone and have to make sense of it using their own intelligence, hampered by a sometimes unrecognised lack of experience. All these novels are set in a society remote from twentieth century England: *The Ennead* is set in an imagined planetary system cir-cling a star named Mnemosyne and is therefore labelled science fiction, while the other two novels are set in no such defined world and so are somewhat arbitrarily labelled fantasy. In all three novels one of the pleasures of reading them derives from the precisely and vividly imagined sense of place. Their landscapes are real and haunting.

Divide and Rule is perhaps the bleakest of these novels and yet the hero, Hanno, is the only central character to be an accepted part of an established and settled family, and therefore he ought to have allies. However, he comes into conflict with established religion (not, of course, Christianity: an invented world allows comment on aspects of this world) and he only recognises the importance of allies when it is too late. Hanno assumes that he has the right to think for himself and has rejected religion; he has turned aside from the traditional path of entry into the family business. Instead he literally and metaphorically rows his own boat and earns a trouble-free basic living as a water-man while still enjoying the benefits of a comfortable home. He is too proud to enlist the sympathy of his family, who assume his choices are completely free, and put up with them because they are fond of him, though in fact he rejected any job involving close work when he realized that his eyesight was deteriorating with terrifying rapidity. He will not accept sympathy; he assumes he is strong enough to stand alone. This can be seen as a portrait of an awkward teenager; it can also be seen as a character embodying the Greek sin of hubris – one whom the gods will bring low.

Indeed, the god does bring Hanno low with remorseless thoroughness. Through the rest of the novel all the freedoms he took for granted are denied him one by one until at the end he is reduced to a homeless, sick and destitute wretch who has lost even his own name, his inner identity. Yet the interesting thing is that Hanno does all this to himself: it is his own determination to rebel and his refusal to back down from his position of scepticism that decides his fate. His impotent anger damages him physically, causing blinding headaches and violent nosebleeds. His determination to cling on to his identity as an individual resisting to the last is precisely what causes the loss of his identity. It is this that makes the novel aesthetically satisfying while at the same time emotionally horrifying.

Hanno is chosen – purely by chance, being of the right age – to be the god's ritual shepherd for a year. The duties are not onerous: he must live in the temple in a special imitation shepherd's hut and be present at the daily service. The position is considered an honourable one and his family is proud of him. After a year he can resume his life.

Hanno, however, is not prepared to compromise and accept what cannot be changed. He is quite unaware at first of the menace that surrounds him, rather despising what he sees as the group of unintelligent believers that he now has to live among, unaware of the strength they have through being numerous, and of his terrifying weakness in being alone and isolated. Where he should seek allies, he makes enemies, and quickly learns of the spitefulness that can masquerade as religion.

Events take a sinister turn. Pettiness turns to menace as Hanno realizes that not only do the temple guards have training in a martial arts technique which renders him physically helpless against a weaker individual, but also that they have no scruples against using this knowledge to commit murder when their religion and therefore livelihood is threatened by growing public apathy. They need a miracle, and construct one by turning the half-mad utterances of a crazed temple hanger-on into prophecies by engineering his death 'without a mark on him' and ensuring he is found by the ritual shepherd. Hanno discovers to his horror that at the very end of his year of office, weakened by ritual fasting and bewildered by changes in the services of the god which everyone around him denies are changes, he must testify to the miracle in public at his final service. His script is written for him. He determines to appear willing but at the final moment to refuse to testify. It is his last mistake: we wish that he would give way and escape the trap, but at the same time we admire the steadfast courage which leads him on in spite of great personal fear: he has been made afraid of water, of the dark, and of the human sacrifice which he discovers was the original lot of the ritual shepherd before these more 'enlightened' times.

Finally at the service he breaks out: 'The god had nothing to do with it!' But how can he prove in public that the god had no hand in killing the crazy temple fool? He hits on a sort of proof: he claims that he himself killed him. Thus he, who always stood for uncompromising truth, has been driven into a lie in an effort not to collude in the corruption of society – and the lie is his undoing. For it is of course claimed to be the god who drove the shepherd to fulfil the prophecy and create the miracle and this marks him out from other ritual shepherds, so that his very name is written into the legend as ritual murderer. Thus he loses his name – ironically, it had irked him all year that everyone called him 'Shepherd' rather than Hanno; now the name Hanno is not safe to use outside the temple, as it is the name of a murderer. His family will not accept him back; he has no friends; he has been utterly broken by the forces of authority and is cast out of the temple, unconscious and entirely alone. We cannot wish Hanno to be different from what he is, and yet being what he is, he must break.

Isaac, the hero of *The Ennead*, is a different proposition: he appears at first to be a survivor. Yet by the end of the novel he is faced with no hope of ultimate escape, as a result of his choice not to collude with a society whose corruption he has belatedly come to recognise. Though he is limited by his narrow experience, the presence in his hostile world of one good character has humanised him, suggesting that in the world of this novel, the individual still counts and hope is still possible.

The third of these remarkable novels, *Aquarius,* is in some ways the strangest of the three. Here again is a young person isolated in hostile surroundings, turned out of his home community on the death of his father, carried downriver by his mother, who soon remarries, rendering him the unwanted stepson in a large family. Even his name, Viner, is a nickname only; he inherits from his dead father the skill of water-divining, but his new community is cursed with too much water and has no use for him. So Viner's very name becomes a term of abuse; the community is superstitious and gullible, does not understand the nature of water-divining and believes that Viner causes the rain that plagues them. Accordingly, as soon as he is old enough he escapes to find a new place where he might be wanted, and a true identity.

The landscape through which he travels is intriguing, perhaps a landscape of the mind: he leaves the wetness behind with amazing rapidity and he begins to use his powers of divining again. He passes ruins and a stone circle and is now in a place of drought where his ability to find water keeps him precariously alive. The story at this point has a compulsive magical quality that draws us on.

Then he meets people – a marauding band of ruffians who talk about killing him, but change their tone once he reveals that he can find water. But these people want only to use him for their own ends; here is a world where the defenceless, such as Viner, are ruthlessly exploited. He is kidnapped and taken blindfold to their country – a country where the king reigns only by virtue of his ability to do the rain dance – only this king is a signal failure: it has not rained for years.

Here is a country which Viner can exploit, as his skill in finding deeply buried water is greatly in demand and he must rise. Gradually he realises that the entire court is as corrupt as the people who brought him here: the palace itself is a vast crumbling facade, cannibalised by succeeding generations: 'a giant's dwelling, yet in it lived people no bigger than himself, like mites in a cheese. The Queen despises her husband, the failed rain-bringer, humiliates him in public and makes it plain that Viner could obtain her hand. At last it seems that Viner has a place in life: recognition, respect and a secure living – everything he was searching for when he left his village.

However, at this point a change occurs in Viner analogous to that in Isaac in *The Ennead*, only in this novel the situation is more complex and the outcome pursued further. Viner finds that he cannot accept the offered majesty – surprisingly, and inconveniently to himself, because of a fellow-feeling growing inside him for the despised and ineffectual king. 'Viner's conscience was new, but it was tender. He was trapped, now.'

He is trapped indeed. Anything which would save the king, notably rain, would hurt Viner. The king's death now would raise Viner as husband of the Queen or new baby princess. How do we ever reconcile rivalry with the desire for friendship?

Viner decides that the only resolution of the conflict is to get the king away and decamp with him. Ironically, the king does not expect, welcome, or even recognize Viner's loyalty. Still, he saves the king from murder and begins an amazing journey through the desert. At last he recognises the terrain and knows his way back to his village, but the king does not wish to accompany him further. Then begins the most astonishing section of the novel. Viner, for a reason which is at first unclear to the reader, imitates what was done to him earlier, kidnaps the distraught king, blindfolds him and forces him across the waste using his baby daughter as hostage. Viner appears to have become as violent and corrupt as the people he despised. He hates himself for what he is doing – especially when he realises how easy it is to prevent passers-by from rescuing the king: all he has to do is explain that he is escorting a madman and everyone avoids them. People believe the captor rather than the captive. Viner has learned much about the workings of the adult world and its identification with those in power.

Viner's motives at this point in the story are an extraordinary (and recognisably adult) mixture of self-seeking and hope for the improvement of society. He has conceived the idea that this king, far from being a king of rain, is a king of drought and does not understand his own nature. He hopes to force him to recognize his powers by making him dance for the rain-drenched villagers and see the sun shine.

The king is nearly overcome by the destruction of all he had lived for: 'I am nothing', he exclaims at one point, echoing the words of characters in the other novels. Viner's will has to serve for them all as by superhuman effort he gets them over the bridge to his village in the greatest storm in human memory. The novel ends with the king constrained to perform what he used to think of as the 'rain' dance, 'dancing in despair beneath the blue sky, the fleeing clouds, the inexorable sun.'

This novel, then, ends with a victory – but what a victory! Reality, like the sun, is pitiless: it demands compromise with virtue, morality, humane feelings, if one is to survive.

The issues raised in all these novels are adolescent issues only in the sense that they are perhaps best appreciated by human beings before they have embarked on the long process of compromise that makes most of us accept and profit from the world we find ourselves in. There are no tacked-on 'happy endings' because these books do not lie about the nature of any universe that contains human beings. The landscapes are as harsh and inexorable as – perhaps – the human soul.

Plainly novels such as these will appeal only to a minority of adolescents, as they do to a minority of adults. The distancing of these stories in space and time helps to draw the reader in, to activate the sense of wonder without which it is difficult to communicate and explore huge and potentially threatening issues. The author shows us young adults facing a world more complicated, and more unpleasant, than they had ever dreamed and thus invites thoughtful adolescents to contemplate the kind of issues which adults find they have to face to get through life.

We need, as Isaac needs, to be accepted into the community – but are there, as he finds, some prices that are too great to pay? Are some things more important than mere survival? Do we have any principles – or if not, how do they develop in us?

How do we cope with a corrupt world? Do we become corrupt too, as Isaac does initially, as Viner almost does, as Hanno (with terrible consequences) refuses to do? In a society where it is impossible to exist without compromise, what sort of compromises are we prepared to make? Do we refuse, like Hanno, and if so, will we lose our very selves, as he does? How can we preserve our identity and sense of self-respect without letting brash overconfidence and pride be our downfall?

How do we find friends and allies in life, and how do we cope with difficulties, like Viner's, of reconciling rivalry and friendship? How do we deal with the great institutions around us whose power is so much greater than ours? If we are to be worth anything as individuals we need to rebel, to strike out our own path in life, as all three characters do. How can we avoid being crushed as they were?

Books referred to in this chapter

(Where my own copy is the paperback, that is the edition I list here.)
Jones, Diana Wynne (1989) *Power of Three*. London: Beaver
Jones, Diana Wynne (1986) *Archer's Goon*. London: Magnet
Jones, Diana Wynne (1981) *The Homeward Bounders*. London: Macmillan
Jones, Diana Wynne (1979) *The Spellcoats*. London: Macmillan
Mahy, Margaret (1989) *Memory*. London: Puffin Plus
Mayne, William (1974) *A Game of Dark*. London: Puffin
Mayne, William (1984) *All the King's Men*. London: Puffin
le Guin, Ursula (1992) *Tehanu*. London: Puffin
Mark, Jan (1990) *Aquarius*. London: Puffin Plus
Mark, Jan (1990) *Divide and Rule*. London: Puffin Plus
Mark, Jan (1989) *The Ennead*. London: Puffin Plus
Ure, Jean (1988) *The Other Side of the Fence*. London: Corgi
Ure, Jean (1990) *One Green Leaf*. London: Corgi

Chapter Twelve

Telly Texts: Children's Books and the Media

Kim Reynolds

Viewers are also Readers

There is a school of thought which holds that books are infinitely and inevitably superior to films and (especially) television, and that any attempt to make a filmed version of a 'good' book (that is, one which critics and/or academics have decreed has literary merit) is doomed to fail. The antipathy to filmed versions of texts is symptomatic of attitudes toward forms of popular culture through the ages, but in the light of cultural and technological changes, such hostility needs to be reconsidered. In particular, the view that watching adaptations of texts is intellectually inferior to reading, and may inhibit reading, is retrograde. As Meek (1991) argues, children are not necessarily passive and indiscriminate viewers, but while looking at visual media may be developing 'visual literacy' skills which can complement and even extend those acquired through more conventional forms of literacy. The ability to decode complex visual narratives precedes, but certainly does not preclude, a similar degree of sophistication and facility with written texts. Indeed, most picture books (which usually constitute the first stage in the process of learning to read printed texts) depend on the child's pre-existing ability to follow visual narratives. Moreover, as is discussed in other chapters, many of the best contemporary picture books draw substantially on narrative techniques developed in other visual media to make an alliance between verbal and visual skills.

Despite the growing body of work which clearly shows that reading and viewing are merely different kinds of literacies, there still exists a vociferous lobby which condemns the practice of adapting books for the media. This attitude was summed up in a review of the BBC's 1992 adaptation of two books in Mary Norton's 'Borrowers' series, *The Borrowers* and *The Borrowers Afield*.

> . . . young people have grown up in a televisual world, and are therefore overwhelmingly susceptible to the influence of pictures. Watching a story requires little mental effort. The child is being denied the opportunity to exercise or develop the imagination . . . Reading fosters mental alertness because it is active; watching is essentially passive. (*The Independent*, 19 November, 1992)

Such diatribes belong to a reactionary discourse which is inappropriate at the multi-media, multi-literate end of the twentieth century. Moreover, this anxiety is cleary misplaced, for far from discouraging children from reading, television and film adaptations have given birth to a vigorous new publishing activity – the book of the film/programme. Indeed, since research first began into the relationship between adaptations and reading it has been shown that broadcast adaptations stimulate reading of the originals and other works by the same author (Himmelweit et al, 1958). In the period 1985–1990 UK children's book sales increased by 170 per cent, precisely the period during which domestic sales of VCRs also peaked and the end of children's reading as a leisure activity was gloomily predicted (*Young Telegraph*, no. 1, 1990). Through TV tie-ins young readers are introduced to an eclectic range of writing, from Ghostbusters to Adrian Mole and back again to such classics as *A Little Princess*, *Ballet Shoes*, *Five Children and It*, *The Chronicles of Narnia*, *Tom's Midnight Garden*, and *The Borrowers*.

The success of adaptations in promoting reading is due to several factors, among them the fact that having seen or heard a version of the text, young readers approach the original with confidence. They know already that they like the story, and they look forward to re-experiencing particularly satisfying moments. Familiarity with the plot enables the viewer-turned-reader to predict what will happen, which is both reassuring and facilitating. Watching and listening can help inexperienced readers by making them familiar with unusual names and specialised or difficult vocabulary. Similarly, viewing a text (or part of a text) before reading it may make new ideas or information more 'reader friendly'; this is particularly true of texts which depend on period settings, objects, and/or historical events. Not the least important aspect of the relationship between reading and viewing is that the child who first encounters a text on television, in the cinema, or on audio tape is almost invariably being introduced to a work which is capable of providing a rich and satisfying reading experience if s/he decides to seek out the original work on which the adaptation was based. Those involved in the costly process of adapting children's books seldom take risks with unknown and untried works. The importance of this kind of introduction to quality fiction in a decade which has experienced unprecedented growth in the production of children's books (in the UK alone more than 5,000 children's books were produced in the fiscal year 1991/2) should not be under-estimated. As librarians, teachers, parents, and booksellers become less and less able to keep abreast of what is published, adaptations of children's books on radio, film, television, or audio tape can at least ensure that large numbers of children are made aware of texts which have been proven to appeal to the majority of young readers.

Many different kinds of adaptations are currently available for children, and the degree to which texts are in fact 'adapted' varies greatly with each. For the purposes of this discussion I am only interested in recorded, re-useable performances, and of these primarily in those adaptations intended for film or television, but it is interesting briefly to compare some of the different ways in which children now encounter adapted texts.

For purists probably the best form of adaptation is the 'complete and unabridged' recording of texts, which in many households now prolongs the nightly ritual of the bedtime story. While such works may not change the words of the original and do not supplement them with pictures as filmed and televised versions do, they are nonetheless adaptations in that they change the medium in which the story was first conceived and marketed, and in the process inevitably alter the relationship between author, narrator, and reader. For instance, the narrator takes on a particular voice (usually that of a well-known actor, often speaking in a cultivated BBC accent), gives personal inflections, and may provide different voices for other characters. Part of the production and editing of such tapes involves adding music for atmospheric purposes. Sound effects also comprise part of the adaptation, and if a work is being serialised for radio, other kinds of technical intervention will affect the child's relationship with the text. For instance, the technique of 'fading out' voices near the end of the chapter may be employed. If the story is being broadcast then the time for listening is predetermined as are the length of the session and the amount of text covered.

A similarly unintrusive form of adaptation is the book read on TV. In such readings the concept of 'book' is even more prominent than in the pre-recorded cassette as the viewer sees the reader holding the book and turning the pages. The camera alternately zooms in on the illustrations and then pulls back to look at whole pages and the reader's face, thereby imitating the child-listener's actions and approximating the one-to-one shared reading experience. Another kind of read-on-TV encounter is provided by the BBC's *Jackanory*, which also involves reading 'real' books on TV but deals with longer books for older readers read over several days.

Over the years the format of this programme has changed considerably, and currently the reader no longer simply sits in a chair and reads aloud from a book, while occasional illustrations fill the screen. The idea that the programme is based on a book is still pre-eminent, but more use is made of the visual nature of television, and television's own narrative conventions. A good example is provided by Victoria Wood's reading of Allan Ahlberg's *Ten in a Bed*. In this adaptation (currently available as a BBC video) considerable use is made of illustrations, which vary greatly from the series of small black and white line drawings by André Amstutz in Ahlberg's original. The large, four-colour illustrations are crudely animated using a series of cutting shots which move from face to face as the characters 'speak'. Each episode begins downstairs, with Victoria Wood pottering around in the kitchen. When it is 'bed-time' she, like Dinah Price, goes up the stairs to the bedroom where the story proper begins. As soon as Dinah Price spies a new fairy-tale character in her bed, Victoria Wood is set spinning in a Dr. Who-style time-travelling whirlpool. The semiotics of this device signal to the viewer that what is happening belongs to another dimension – presumably the dimension of fantasy. Thus the transition between reality and fantasy is highlighted in a way which departs significantly from Ahlberg's text, which maintains a consistently matter-of-fact tone throughout.

Thus far none of the modes of adaptation discussed involves altering the text substantially, and most have deliberately called attention to the fact that what the viewer or listener is experiencing began life in book form. However, adapatations which take the form of performances on film and TV raise a new set of issues and problems. It is recorded performances of texts which are most likely to incur the wrath of the anti-adaptation brigade. Performances are criticised on the grounds that they simplify complex narratives, prohibit the child from creating his/her own fantasy worlds because the visual impact of the performance is overwhelming and indelible, that the compression of a book which may take several days to read into 90 minutes (or less) diminishes its impact, and so on.

To explore these issues adequately it is necessary to look in detail at the adaptation process. Of course, there are many kinds of adaptations, but the specific problems posed for the adaptors by different kinds of books (for instance, picture books and novels, fantasies and autobiographies, detective stories and romances) are of less importance here than more basic considerations. The most important of these early decisions has traditionally been whether the adaptation should consist of a single, feature-length performance, or whether it should be serialised over several episodes, usually broadcast in a weekly slot. Each has its advantages, but many have favoured adaptations in serial form for two reasons. First, serialised adaptations are given more viewing time overall, and so may need to simplify texts less than do single performances. The second advantage of the serial is that its inevitable interruptions often encourage readers to move from screen to text to find out what happens next. The desire to read ahead is frequently stimulated by the serials' dependence on 'cliff-hanger' endings, designed to encourage viewers to tune in again for the next episode. When viewers become readers between episodes, their relationship with screened adaptations is altered considerably.

While many children's texts are first adapted and broadcast in serial form, most are now also conceived with the home video market in mind. This means that ultimately most viewers will see the adaptations as single, continuous performances which they can watch many times. For this reason it is important to consider the relationship between video viewing and texts before looking in detail at a representative adaptation.

The Video and the Viewer

When viewed on a VCR, filmed adaptations of books are not just useful for entertaining children; they have the potential to make the viewing process more analogous to reading and so to developing analytical skills useful for both activities. VCRs make it possible to re-view, to skim, to watch selected scenes repeatedly, to omit sections and pause over others, to resume viewing after interruptions – all of which make viewing more personal, more creative, and potentially more intellectually demanding.

The ramifications of this degree of control over visual adaptations are many. Older children may benefit from the very detailed interaction it affords between written and visual texts. By encouraging visual decoding, videos may enhance understanding of a director's version of a text and so the potential for comparison with the reader's own interpretation. Repeated watching of a visual version of a text with which the child is familiar can highlight differences in the narrative functioning and capabilities of the two media. Even a young child will notice and understand adjustments to the way in which a story is told: for instance, the need to make the narrator a character in the action or to substitute enactments for descriptions of events (as in a letter). By comparing the narrative organisation of printed and visual versions of texts, a great deal can be learned about the relationship between structure, form, and meaning.

Probably the most contentious aspect of adaptations is the tendency to compromise endings and crises for juvenile audiences, and even to alter them in ways which seem to contradict the original intention. The quintessential example of this kind of adjusted ending is provided by the 1988 film version of Robert Cormier's deeply troubling book, *The Chocolate War* (1974). The book ends ambiguously, with the central character, Jerry Renault, seriously injured – perhaps dying – after a maliciously manipulated boxing match. He struggles to explain to his friend Goober what he has learned through the weeks of his ordeal with the Vigils: that it is pointless to 'disturb the universe', and that there is no divine justice. The novel is bleakly pessimistic, challenging the vigorously disseminated American dream that every citizen counts and the individual prepared to take a just moral stand is a hero. By contrast, the film shows Jerry winning the boxing match, vanquishing his tormentor, the arch-manipulator, Archie, and idealised as the champion of the school (significantly, the film also makes it clear that this is no moral victory and that Jerry, while technically the victor, has in fact lost the larger fight).

The practice of glossing over unhappy endings is open to criticism, and needs to be examined by those responsible for adapting books written for young readers. Adaptations such as *The Chocolate War* may lend fuel to those who feel that the literary text is sacrosanct and that adaptations, if they must be made, should have total fidelity to the text as their ruling principle. In fact, as I have argued elsewhere, adapations which are governed by total fidelity are often ineffective, and if one of the desired outcomes of adaptations is to introduce viewers to literary texts, then the need to simplify plots and sometimes to adjust endings may be regarded as a good thing. The viewer-turned-reader who finds the original text more rich, complex, thought-provoking and satisfying than the adaptation will have a good reading experience, which is demonstrably the best way to make keen readers. Moreover, often when a reader returns to a filmed version of the text, 'happy' endings turn out to be more ambiguous than they first appeared. This is certainly true of the adaptation of Cormier's book, which actually deals with the same issues of compromise and failure in different ways. It is less physically violent, but the emotional impact is equally devastating. Moreover, the filmed version reflects knowledge of the book's sequel, and so opens out towards debates Cormier later develops.

The Popular Series Adapted: Enid Blyton's *The Castle of Adventure*

In each of the examples discussed above, the relationship between books and screened adaptations seems to be complementary and productive, for even very young readers/viewers will be aware of and curious about changes to the stories they know, and can benefit greatly from comparing and asking questions about the different versions. However, all of the adaptations considered so far are based on texts which are highly regarded in the juvenile canon for the range and complexity of the issues they raise as well as for stylistic innovations. What happens to the relationship between original and adaptation when the text itself is deliberately simplistic and preoccupied with providing entertaining reading rather than with literary status? Enid Blyton has been the exemplar of children's recreational reading for much of this century, and the 1990 TVS adaptation of *The Castle of Adventure* illustrates well the problems and possibilities of adapting less intellectually challenging books.

Blyton's series of 'Adventure' books, featuring the tufty-haired Mannering children and their red-haired and freckled live-in companions, orphans Jack and Lucy Ann Trent, first began to appear in the 1940s. *The Castle of Adventure*, published in 1946, the second in the series, was adapted for television nearly half a century later. It is in many way a successful adaptation in that the scriptwriter and production team were more concerned with fidelity to the experience of the text than they were with slavishly attempting to follow the story as Blyton wrote it. Thus the film version sets out to draw the reader in to a fast-paced and exciting narrative in which justice prevails, children are cleverer than villains, and right adult authority is reassuringly present and effective when necessary.

Unlike the BBC 'classic serials' treatment typified by *The Chronicles of Narnia* and *The Borrowers*, the TVS team were not interested in the period flavour characteristic of Blyton's work. Indeed, the adaptation brings the text up to date; Mrs. Mannering and the four children no longer belong to the 1940s middle-class world of porters, trains, books and luncheons. Boarding schools, the constant other world in the lives of these adventuring children, are pushed firmly to the background. The film begins with the children and Mrs. Mannering (in the book a youngish, pretty widow, played in the film by Susan George as a glamorous single parent cautiously in pursuit of a partner) arriving at their holiday cottage in a bright, red, family hatch-back. Whereas the book, in keeping with many other serials written in the first half of the century, pays little attention to differences in the age and sex of characters and shows the four as an extremely tight-knit group, the film is very conscious of the unlikely nature of such a band in 1990. Thus Phillip and Jack, both roughly fifteen years old, are clearly adolescent and reluctant to 'play' with their younger sisters until the adventure really gets under way.

Other changes have also been made for modern audiences. A computer game had found its way into the holiday cottage, the children pretend they think the spies they discover are operating a pirate radio station, and Bill Cunningham, their adult companion in adventures, clearly belongs to the post-James Bond world of espionage rather than the vague but powerful and unashamedly patriotic and ideological position he occupies in the book. Modern sensibilities are also catered to. For instance, Blyton's original betrays struggles with ambivalent feelings towards Tassie, the gypsy girl who helps the four children at different stages in the adventure. Being English-born, Tassie does not fall into the entirely dubious category of 'foreigner', but her gypsy blood is obviously a handicap in Blyton's eyes, and she has Mrs. Mannering scrub her with carbolic soap before she's happy for the children to associate with her. Although Blyton makes several attempts to suggest that Tassie is different rather than despicable, she nonetheless slips into a disapproving mode whenever she dwells on her for any length of time. For instance, the narrator observes that Tassie is 'more like an intelligent animal than a little girl'; Blyton has Tassie climb through the window for breakfast like one of Phillip's tame pets, and, along with other 'creatures', she is devoted to Phillip. The film avoids any such contentious issues; its treatment of Tassie is politically correct in every way. She is well cared for though uneducated, clean, and capable. She has also been transformed from the little girl of the text to a rebellious teenager, aware of the vaguely sexual threats which keep her mother under the control of the wicked Sam, a character entirely invented for the film.

Blyton's story-telling technique is alternately condemned and praised for its simplicity (not a surprising quality in a writer who was capable of producing a 50,000 word book in five days). While many educationists have agonised over the lack of literary quality (among other things!) in her books, Aidan Chambers suggests that this is precisely what makes them so successful with children:

> . . . her simplistic plots, her basic, undecorated and clichéd language and characters leave children free to embroider and enrich her stories *in their own way*. Blyton provides an outline on which to graft . . . refinements. (Ingham, 1982)

Moreover, the formulaic nature of Blyton's stories enables even the young and inexperienced reader quickly to be able to predict endings, identify villains, and relax in the knowledge and security provided by the formula. Given these attributes, most of which characterize all forms of popular writing, the relationship between books such as *The Castle of Adventure* and their adaptations seems to be more problematic than is the case for more complex originals.

The problem lies in the very simplicity of the text, and it is problematic in at least two ways. Most obviously, if the text is simple, operating primarily at the level of plot, then there is very little for the reader to discover when moving from adaptation to text. A simple linear narrative can easily be reproduced on film, and the satisfaction of re-experiencing the story may easily be destroyed by comparing the exciting, high-tech world on the screen with the more basic settings in the book. As Chambers points out, the real pleasure for readers of Enid Blyton is that her work requires them to fill in the gaps, to dramatise and enrich what are essentially good plots. Accordingly, the hermeneutic processes reading involves are less mediated by the text and so more directly personal. Such texts, better than any others, illustrate that what is being read is not just the text, but the self. What makes the text satisfying is what the reader brings to a given reading. If, through having seen a visually exciting adaptation, blueprints such as those provided by Blyton become too detailed and concrete, there are fewer opportunities for readers to insert themselves into the text, and the text becomes less able to function as a covert form of wish-fulfilment. The best examples of this loss in relation to *The Castle of Adventure* can be seen in the characters of Kiki the parrot and Phillip Mannering.

In the Adventure series, Kiki is at least as much a character as any of the children. Her remarkable powers of imitation often result in hilarious incidents, but just as often are called upon to save the children from imminent disaster. She is cheeky to teachers, governesses, and most forms of authority, treating them exactly as the children in the book (and, no doubt, those reading it) wish to – she is the child's repressed, subversive voice. Phillip represents a different form of power for the young reader. His power over animals (anything from slow worms to wolves, bears, and poisonous snakes) embodies several common wishfulfilment fantasies at once. First, it plays upon the natural affinity between children and animals, and children's common desire for animals to love and respect them. In part the need to be loved by animals and to have power over them comes from the child's need to be recognised as lovable, powerful and special. Phillip's power is particularly satisfying as he can do what most adults cannot.

In the adaptation of Blyton's book both Kiki and Phillip have inevitably become pale imitations of their book-selves. The mode in which the adaptation is filmed is predominantly naturalistic (with elements of farce surrounding the villains). Accordingly Phillip is portrayed as just a boy who likes creatures and carries the odd frog around in his pocket, while Kiki is an all-too-real parrot whose voice could never be mistaken for a human's and whose repertoire of sounds is limited to the occasional squawk. Whether, having seen these two characters on the screen, the child reader will be able to accept their extraordinary powers on the page is debatable.

Conclusion

Adaptation is not a new phenomenon – good stories have always been re-told in every available medium. Before film and television there were stage adaptations of many novels, and authors themselves often adapted scenes from novels to make short public readings. For the juvenile audience, adaptations have the virtues of introducing books to children and facilitating the transition to longer narratives. Taken together, particularly using video technology, adaptations and texts can be mutually enhancing, raising a wide range of issues, from those to do with style, form and structure, to those concerned with what happens and why. Adaptations may be the only way of bringing non-readers into contact with the kinds of stories which can enlarge personal and social understanding. For good readers, the pleasures of the written text will never be superseded, though they may well be extended by, the pleasures of the screen.

The real question is not *whether* to adapt, but *how* and *what* to adapt. There is a growing video library of adaptations for children, many of which are thoughtful and true to the story lines of the original texts. If this library is to help develop children's literacy skills of every kind, however, it needs to move beyond the preoccupation with textual fidelity and to learn to exploit the visual medium, be it film or television, of the adaptation. This is important because no matter how good the adaptation, there will always be aspects of literary texts (unlike those typified by *The Castle of Adventure*, in which sensational plots predominate) which cannot be shown in the conventional sense. This is because such works tend to be concerned with exploring internal states, providing ancillary information, and generally digressing from the main action of the text. At present too many adaptations try to pretend that they *are* books. It would be exciting to see producers and dramatists of books for children capitalising on the possibilities inherent in children's reading *and* viewing habits to tackle the adaptation process in more imaginative ways. This can only stimulate children's interest in the original texts, and in the process develop the natural alliance between verbal and visual literacy in the next generation of reader-viewers.

Chapter Thirteen

Meg Meets the Turtles: Whose Books Count in Primary Classrooms?

Alison Kelly

Children's earliest literacy learning takes place in a broad landscape within which books are only one part. The narratives and characters from television and video have a hugely significant impact on children's lives. So too does the environmental print that they encounter in many different contexts – at the supermarket, on television, and at mealtimes (the Macdonalds logo is a much-quoted piece of such early learning!). These influences and contexts overlap so 'My Little Pony' preens herself on plastic lunch boxes and 'Teenage Mutant Hero Turtles' leap across packets of juice. Both play a role in establishing children's first understanding of what reading is all about.

When children come to school they continue to learn about the practices and customs of reading. Shirley Brice Heath's (1983) ethnographic study contrasted two communities in the United States and revealed a possible tension between what children learn at home and what is then expected of them in school. For example, she describes how the children from one of the communities, Trackton, 'lived in a flow of time' (p.275) where they initiated and carried out play activities quite independently. On arriving at preschool they were perplexed to find that there was 'a time to sit down, a time to listen, a time to draw . . .' The school's practices around story were especially confusing for these children who were soaked in a very particular story telling culture which actively encouraged exaggeration and elaboration while

> Inside the classroom, their language play, incorporation of commercial characters, and many of their themes are unacceptable. (p.297)

Heath describes the teachers' ambivalence when the children tried to 'take the floor' at story time (p.280). This chattering and storying that they had learnt from their community's practices was suddenly no longer appropriate.

The importance of children's experience prior to school has become an acceptable tenet of primary practice. The Cox Report (1989), (which provided the foundations for the Programmes of Study and Attainment Targets for English) exhorts us to build from this basis (para 16.8); the nationally (and internationally) used *Primary Language Record* (1988) includes as a vital element a parent/teacher conference which allows for dialogue about children's out-of-school learning and interests. I am concerned however that all of the insights gained from such discussions should be seen as useful. We may learn that a child enjoys video cartoons, seeks out Turtle comics, can distinguish Raphael from Leonardo by the inital on the belt but we may not know how best to use this in the classroom. It is all too easy to fall into the trap of 'celebrating away' (Buckingham, 1990) around children's popular culture without sufficient critical reflection.

Invariably we present the children with what we would describe as a rich and wonderful selection of picture books that form the backbone of an unofficial primary canon; its authors include John Burningham, Anthony Browne, Pat Hutchins and the Ahlbergs. Typical features of this 'canon' are a structured and meaningful narrative which may be patterned or repetitive, and a polysemic layering of meaning (cf Chapter 2) often achieved through the juxtaposition of text and image. These are all marvellous authors whose reading lessons for children have been defined for us with such clarity by Margaret Meek (1988) in her 'workshop' *How Texts Teach What Readers Learn*. I would always have them in my classroom. But is it a selection that goes far enough?

In addition to ensuring that the books in our classrooms provide the enticement and challenge that young readers need, teachers also confront the difficulty of providing books that are not overtly racist or sexist. It is not the intention of this piece to pursue the arguments in this troubled area of 'political correctness' with the attention they deserve but the fact is that many of the texts drawn from children's popular culture are both racist and sexist; the difficulty then is that well-founded anxieties about equal opportunities may be asserted against the children's own cultural experience.

My interest lies with those classroom moments where differing interests intersect to create new conjunctions of text and image. When children are given the opportunity to draw from the wider landscape – one that reaches beyond the 'good' books in the book corner – then maybe the place for a broader range of texts can be articulated.

James' story, *Meg Meets the Turtles*, (Figure 13.1) is just one example

Figure 13.1

of a successful merger of texts from within and without school. His teacher had suggested he make a book for the class about Teenage Mutant Hero Turtles (an overwhelming preoccupation for both him and many of the boys in the class at that time). With a sure sense of the rather complex audience demands of such a suggestion (pleasing teacher and peers) he chose to construct a story around the meeting of Meg from the *Meg and Mog* books by Jan Pienkowski) and a Turtle.

On the first page (Figure 13.2) there is, as any Turtle afficionado will know, a sewer lid. However, our attention is drawn to it subtly by the disappearance of Meg's hat out of the top frame of the picture. Now it could be that, at this point, the unconfident reader fears an unskilful illustrator who has misjudged the space, but this fear is quickly banished on the next page (Figure 13.3) which reveals the almost symmetrical appearance and disappearance of Michelangelo and Meg respectively. There is a wonderful tension in page 3 (Figure 13.4) between a bland and understated text 'They get out of the drain. Meg flies to say Hello' with the powerful swooping image of Meg pitched against the weapon-primed Turtle who, unsurprisingly, backs out of page 4's (Figure 13.5) frame looking glum. Off her broomstick on page 5 (Figure 13.6) but still with her arms outstretched (making a spell?), she is smiling and we discover why on page 6 (Figure 13.7) as she entices Michelangelo back into the frame with a chicken and a party (Figure 13.8) thus providing a happy ending.

James' book is a skilful manipulation of both picture book and media conventions. He uses the edges of the pictures dramatically and tantalisingly to sustain a flow and continuity of action. This skilful framing of the action surely owes much to his understanding of cartoons. He reveals authorial skills too in the unspoken tension created through the balance between text and pictures and the presentation of familiar characters from other contexts. These are skills learned from the likes of Burningham, the Ahlbergs and Browne.

Children's expertise about media characters is fed by many different sources. Their prime concern is probably with the television lives of these characters but they are also absorbed by the many skilfully marketed artefacts (games, figures, food, bubble bath, back-packs, cards etc). Their talk, their drawing and most importantly their play are often dominated by these characters.

It is their play to which I now turn as it is most likely that James' control of media narratives came in on a wave of his own play both at home and school. Barrs (1988) has shown us just how significant this can be. She describes a five-year-old's play centred on Star Wars and Masters of the Universe and explains that media narratives:

Figure 13.2

the TURTLES
Lit up the
drain

Figure 13.3

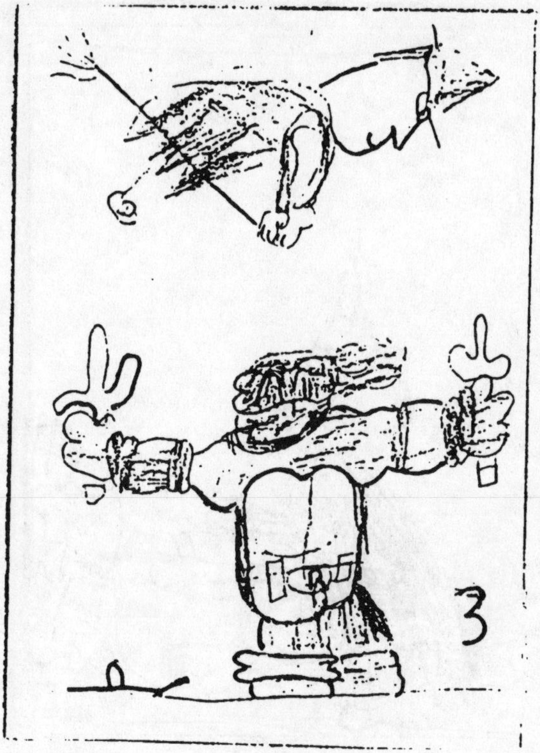

Theyget outof tendrin
Meg filcs to say
Hello

Figure 13.4

The TVrtles were frightened

Figure 13.5

Figure 13.6

Figure 13.7

Figure 13.8

which are such powerful influences on dramatic play will also affect the development of children's sense of story, their narrative expectations and eventually their own written narratives – in other words their literary development (p.102)

Barrs draws from Vygotsky's (1978) arguments to show how, for young children, the role of play (and drawing) is critical to their development of understanding about symbolic representation, an understanding which is needed in order to underpin their later moves into writing. This is important when we think about the opportunities for role play in early years classrooms, particularly for the responses we, as teachers, make to the incorporation of media characters into such play. In her inspiring chronicle of work in a kindergarten, Vivian Gussin Paley (1981) writes of Wally's enthusiasm for Superhero play:

He loved to playact Superman and Han Solo, and he told enough of these stories to keep his membership in the brotherhood active. (p.130)

The honesty with which Paley discusses the gendered differences between the children's stories and play in this book and in *Boys and Girls* is a most helpful and practical contribution in this area.

The central example of this chapter is that of a boy and his current media heroes. There have been many criticisms of the violence in the Turtles yet James draws from two different traditions to present this most benign, even momentarily scared, Turtle. But the presentation of such a positive reconstruction should not be used to minimise the problem. As I write, Turtles have been superseded by the wrestlers of the World Wrestling Federation – neither present a very optimistic vision for women or girls! Nevertheless children's popular culture is here to stay, and whether we impose bans in school or not children will remain absorbed by it. Girls have their heroes and heroines too but, occuring as they do in the shape of Care Bears or My Little Pony, there is little to reassure us that the balance is being addressed, let alone redressed. I must however argue for their place in school both in terms of developing literacy and also for the encouragement of children's own critical stance. If we do not allow these stories into the classroom at all how can we enable children to stand back from them, to reflect on them and manipulate them? Paley's apposite remark that 'I, the teacher, am not a princess and need not act as if the superheroes will pull down the classroom walls.' (1984, p.116) is a timely reminder of the teacher's role in all this – a role that goes beyond 'celebrating away'.

Gillian Lathey (1988) writes convincingly about her work with Years 1 and 2 children in which she both permitted and encouraged their inclusion of media figures in drawing and writing. She identifies the difficulties about 'crudeness and over-emphasis on violence' but concludes that:

I have found that in a context where their culture is accepted and discussed, children will eventually reach a stage in their writing where they take control of media figures. (p.58)

The inclusion of media education in the English National Curriculum endorses the importance of developing this critical stance so that children can learn to stand back from and to inspect the images of their culture. Children are not, after all passive ciphers of popular culture. As Paley noted, the boundaries between fantasy and reality were clearly understood and maintained by the children:

When real events and problems were considered, no one mentioned Superman. Even the boys, whose absorption in this play dominated the sound waves, knew the difference between play and real influence. A powerful and exciting superhero could not move a bag of sand or make a wish come true. (p.131)

James reworks narratives and images from home and school; his book is poised to meet the needs and expectations of his audience and also reveals the potential of such learning episodes. I believe that if we base our teaching solely on just one view of 'good books' this may be doubly disempowering, as it can exclude the children's own experience and expertise and the opportunity to yield and manipulate the complex skills learnt from a diverse range of influences. Meek (1992) says that 'the intensely-felt early experiences of children . . . become engagements with literary texts ' (p.2). The recognition that children's popular culture may well be amongst these earliest experiences is crucial. So too is the acknowledgement that the manipulation of media figures in play and writing may be important and empowering for children.

(I would like to thank James for letting me borrow his book. I would also like to acknowledge my gratitude to his teacher, Sue Coller – her classroom was an inspiration.)

E

Chapter Fourteen

Story and the Development of Children's Language and Literacy

Mary Walsh

I became aware of, and interested in, the power of story when my own children were very young. Stories became as much a part of their everyday life as eating and drinking. As they progressed through their primary school, I watched them benefit from their pre-school exposure to books and story, and become readers for life.

As a special needs teacher in a London Borough primary school, it became increasingly obvious to me that the children experiencing difficulties in reading and writing were often those who had little or no pre-school experience of stories and books. Some were also victims of strictly regulated reading schemes with little emphasis on real stories and books.

Convinced of the power of story and the use of real story books in the development of children's literacy skills, I decided to do my own investigation with a group of eight six-year old children who needed extra help with reading and writing. They were all on the *One, Two Three and Away!* reading scheme but were not reading with fluency or for meaning; some were only able to recognise a few words. Not surprisingly, they lacked interest in books and were also reluctant to make attempts at writing.

My principal aim was to investigate the value of story in the development both of children's literacy and of their positive attitudes to books and reading.

I decided, therefore, to expose these children to a great deal of story, reading stories to them on a regular basis. I abandoned the use of the reading scheme on which they appeared to be failing and started using a story book approach to reading, using the *Story Chest* scheme. I also observed the children's writing development as their exposure to story gradually encouraged them to write and to develop positive attitudes to writing. As the study developed I began to notice changes in their attitudes to reading and writing and improvements in their performance in these areas.

The Story-reading Sessions

From the beginning of these regular sessions, the children were very receptive to hearing stories, despite their current negative attitudes to books and reading.

Books with a great deal of repetition and rhyme encouraged the children to join in. By picking up phrases such as '. . . or I'll hit you with my bommy-knocker' (in *The Hungry Giant*), they were soon able to read many of the stories along with me. At times I read them some poems from *Animal Nonsense Rhymes* which they found very amusing. This led to various rhyming games. At the beginning of the year I was amazed how unaware some of the children were of the more famous nursery rhymes. One did not know 'Three Blind Mice' and another had never heard of 'Little Miss Muffett', so I tried to use many books with rhyme and repetition, including nursery rhymes.

As the children listened to real stories, they started to pick up the language of books and the conventions of story language such as popular beginning and endings. Illustrations also attracted their attention; when I read *Boggity-Bog* they made comments like 'Miss, look at his motor bike' and 'that snail is squashed' without any initial questions from me.

The children also started to relate what I read to their own experiences. The story of *The Old Oak Tree* developed into a discussion about conkers, and one child, Claire, informed the group 'At Lincolnshire [where she had been a few weeks previously] they've got conkers.' *The Hungry Giant* led to a discussion about their experiences of bee-stings and *Winnie The Witch*, who gets angry and red in the face, caused Michael to tell the group how his baby sister did the same when crying.

When I read *Not Now, Bernard*, in which Bernard's parents constantly ignore him, even failing to notice when he is devoured by a monster, Darren quickly identified with Bernard saying:

> 'My mum doesn't talk to me. I told my mum that a dog bit me and she doesn't listen.'

It was not long before the children started using what they heard to interconnect with other stories. For example, when I read the *The Princess and the Frog*, they began discussing the meaning of the word 'sternly'. When Daniel said it meant 'angry', Paul quickly added, 'like the Hungry Giant'.

As the children engaged in more discussion and became more confident about speaking, their oral fluency improved. My observations in this respect would support the research of Wells (1982) which found that children who were read to and shared stories with adults were more advanced in their oral language development than those who did not have this experience. The children also became better at listening to each other and asking each other questions. They began to feel confident that what they had to say was of value.

In the second term, I noticed that the children were becoming more discriminating in their response to the stories. In the early weeks, if asked whether or not they had enjoyed a story, they would all say yes but would not offer much more information. However, later, when I read *The Princess and the Frog*, they were very clear about which parts of the story they enjoyed:

> Paul: 'I liked when they got married.'
> Sean: 'I liked when she was crying and she was in the bed.'
> Daniel: 'I liked the bit when the frog jumped into the water and got the ball.'

The children gradually became more discriminating about stories and books in general. Nicola told me:

> 'I liked all the story books except I don't like Turtle books.'
> Claire, during the same discussion, informed me:
> 'I don't like the stories that are very long.'

The children began to want to buy books; after hearing *The Tiger Who Came To Tea*, Nicola said, 'I wish I could get it in the bookshop'. She had never previously been a customer at the school bookshop.

Books brought in by the children also gave good opportunities for discussion. Paul brought in *Teddy Takes A Train* which was in rhyme form. Although I did not like the book at first, it led to the news that Sean had gone to a museum and seen a steam train 'of the olden days'. Daniel then told us about his trip to Nigeria on an aeroplane. The same story also initiated a great deal of talk about funfairs, obviously bringing back memories of their own experiences. Daniel noticed that Teddy was 'covering his eyes' on the roller coaster and could understand why. Using this book with the children proved to me that teachers may not always be the best judges of what children will gain from a particular book. Without exception, the children were very pleased when I read their own books to the group. I believe it made them feel as if their books were just as valuable as the ones I myself chose to read.

Gradually the children were beginning to predict what might happen in stories and to engage in problem-solving. When *Winnie The Witch* changed the cat from black to many different colours to avoid tripping over him,

Paul cried, 'I knew it!'. Michael, on hearing that the cat had gone into the grass after being changed to green, declared:

'She'll fall over him 'cos the cat is green.'

The element of magic in this story and in others such as *The Magic Porridge Pot* always seemed to attract and hold the attention of the children and often made them keen to write. When I read *Burglar Bill*, the children were intrigued and could not understand how Bill could have stolen a bed. The following conversation ensued:

Darren: 'How did he steal a bed?'
Daniel: 'Maybe he had a van.'
Paul (introducing the magical element): 'He only had a sack. He must have made it small and then made it big when he got home.'
Sean: 'He might have stolen it in pieces'
Paul: 'and fixed it when he got home.'

They all agreed that this last suggestion was most likely how Bill had stolen the bed. They had solved the problem between them.

Fairy stories often led the children to the discussion of moral issues. (This recalls what Susan Fremantle describes in Chapter 6). In *The Princess and the Frog*, they felt the princess was acting unfairly when she refused to keep her promise to the frog. They laughed when *The Hungry Giant* got stung by the bees and felt this was just punishment for treating the people badly. In *A Barrel Of Gold*, where a foolish burglar gets bitten by a dog, the children were adamant that he deserved his fate because he had shouted while trying to steal the gold. The story *Burglar Bill* led to a discussion about the morality of stealing for a living rather than working. In the same story the children were pleased when Bill finally got married. They felt he deserved happiness because he had returned all he had stolen. Obviously the story appealed to their moral development – the idea that all will work out well for those who repent and make amends. I would suggest that, by confronting the children with basic human problems such as crime and evil, story was contributing to their inner growth and their psychological and personal development.

Stories also enabled the children to name and talk about certain anxieties and emotions. (This reiterates the points made by Nicola Humble in Chapter 8). After reading *The Owl Who Was Afraid Of The Dark*, Darren admitted that he was afraid of the dark. Only through identifying with the owl in the story was he able to talk about his anxieties. The children talked about various emotions, including happiness, sadness, loneliness, isolation, injustice and fear. They were not afraid of fairy stories which presented violent or frightening people or events. Through story, they were able to confront problems similar to their own but, as the Bullock Report

(1975) stresses, 'at the safety of one remove.'

It was interesting to see how much fun and excitement the children got from being read to. They laughed a great deal when the burglar in *A Barrel Of Gold* got bitten by the dog who ran off with some of his trousers in his mouth. They found *Can You Hear Me, Grandad*? particularly funny and could not wait to write about it and draw some of the amusing illustrations. In the story, Grandad is deaf and always mistakes what his granddaughter says. There is a great emphasis on rhyme. For example, when the girl says she's going to have a ride on the llamas, he thinks she says she's going to the zoo in her pyjamas. It was not long before they knew the story off by heart and were making up their own rhyming alternatives.

Thus it can be seen that stories help children to find meaning as well as enriching their experience and helping to stimulate their imagination. The children became really involved in the stories they heard and wanted to read some of them for themselves as well as to draw and write about them. Their everyday lives were enriched because, through listening to and reading stories, they were able to have experiences which they might not otherwise have been able to have. Their lively conversations also seemed to help them to organize their thoughts, feelings and experiences. This type of discussion was contributing to the children's cognitive development, helping them to categorize information and to move from concrete actions to abstract thought.

The Reading Development of the Children

The children were excited when I changed them from the *One, Two, Three and Away!* books to the *Story Chest* books. Initially some of them were overwhelmed and found the element of choice difficult. Being able to choose from such a large number of books was a big change for them. At first I found it easier to suggest a few that they might like to choose from. Before long, I noticed them developing an interest in reading. It was extremely encouraging to observe their growing enjoyment and sense of fun and excitement connected with stories and books. Reading began to be something they chose to do for a purpose, essentially enjoyment. The stories they heard made them more motivated to read stories for themselves. Some of the parents were beginning to make the same observations and to notice a change in their children's attitudes at home. I will focus here on the reading development of one particular child, Paul.

Paul was having great difficulties with the *One, Two, Three and Away!* scheme. In fact he could only recognise the words 'I' and 'a'. I changed him to *Story Chest* at the beginning of the period and soon he was enjoying the new books. Paul's mother was very supportive and he shared a book with her every night. At a parents' evening in the Autumn Term she talked about the difference the new approach was already making to Paul's attitude to reading. She explained that reading had been a chore while he was on the other scheme. Every night she had been having a battle with him to get him to read a page or two. Now, it was Paul who would remind her that he had to read. When asked later why he didn't enjoy the *One, Two, Three and Away!* books he explained that they

> 'don't have no funny stories. They have about Billy Blue Hat and Roger Red Hat'

It was obvious when I started sharing books with Paul that he had a very poor knowledge of rhyme and knew very few of the common nursery rhymes. I began to use some nursery rhyme books with him; he enjoyed them a great deal and would often choose one to take home.

By the middle of the next term, Paul was becoming very involved in story and would listen to and pick up stories and rhymes while other children were reading their books. He was also starting to become discriminating about books. One day when one of the children was reading *The Old Oak Tree* Paul told me:

> I like that because they've got big feet. That's one of my favourites – that one and The Hungry Giant.

If another child was reading a book that Paul had already read, Paul was always bursting to tell the other child what the story was all about.

At this time Paul was also beginning to look at other books in the room. He would often show a particular book to others in the group and in no time they would all gather round and look together, studying the pictures and talking about the book.

By the end of the school year, Paul had read nearly all of the books in the Story Chest Stage 1 with me and was well on the way to becoming an independent reader. He was beginning to recognise words and use picture cues and initial sound strategies. He was now getting a great deal of meaning from books. His whole attitude to books and reading had become very positive. He loved books and saw himself as a reader. If another child was reading a book which he had already read he would often say:

> 'I've read that. That's any easy book.'

At a parents' meeting, Paul's mother told me that he was choosing other books to read at home and would always have a go even if he chose a difficult book.

The reading development of three other children in the group followed a similar pattern to that of Paul. They developed positive attitudes to books and reading and got a great deal of meaning out of what they read.

Although they were not yet reading independently at the end of the year they too were well on the way to doing so.

Three more of the children did become independent readers and were on Stages 3/4 of Story Chest at the end of the school year by which time they were reading much more fluently and with enjoyment and meaning.

The Writing Development of the Children

At the beginning of the school year, all the children were reluctant to write. As we read stories they had plenty to say about them and could retell what had happened but they were unable to write anything down. I therefore decided to let them dictate their stories to me and I would write them out and let them copy under my writing. As they became interested in the stories they were reading and having read to them, they became keen to draw pictures and write stories. They knew I would write out their own stories for them and this made them less inhibited. It was not until the second term that most the children made their first attempts at writing independently. Once again I will focus in particular on the development of Paul.

Paul had greater problems with writing than the others. He took much longer to learn letter names and sounds and was the child with the least concept of rhyme. Paul was seen earlier in the year by the educational psychologist with a view to obtaining extra specialist help through the full assessment procedure. It was a while before Paul had the confidence to begin to write independently. I continued to write out his stories for him until February when, after hearing *A Barrel Of Gold*, he attempted his own writing (Figure 14.1). He was so pleased with his attempt that he continued with independent writing after that and in March made an excellent attempt to retell the story of *The Sunflower That Went FLOP* (Figure 14.2). Paul's confidence in writing went from strength to strength and in June he wrote some interesting news about the funfair (Figure 14.3) which showed considerable improvement. About a week after Paul wrote this, I was complimenting another child on one of her stories and Paul confidently interrupted saying: 'I'm quite good at stories too.' Paul was beginning to see himself as a writer as well as a reader. A visit from the educational psychologist later in the year brought the encouraging news that, due to his continued progress in reading and writing, Paul would no longer need to go through the statementing procedure.

My observations showed that while the children were exposed to a great deal of story and books, they developed a more positive attitude to writing. They began to enjoy writing and became keen to write stories. Their writing began to improve and become more interesting as they became less inhibited by the conventions of spelling and more interested in what they

Mond ay 25th February
The Burglar and the gold.
The Burglar and the gold.

n w in to th has.

a t g the gold. ✓ very
                        good

he went in to the house.

and he got the gold.

Figure 14.1 *One of Paul's first attempts at independent writing (February).* Paul wrote this after hearing the story, *A Barrel Of Gold*. (Notice he decided on a different title which he asked me to write out first for him.) Underneath I have written down what he said when he read it back to me.

Monday, 18th March
THe Sunflower that went FLOP

FLop we the sunflower
and it wit ewhear
and it and r the ✓ good boy!
and it stop

Flop went the sunflower
and it went everywhere
and it rained and rained
and it was straight.

Figure 14.2 *Paul's version of The Sunflower That Went FLOP (March).*
Paul wrote this independently after hearing this story. Underneath, I have
written down what he said when he read it back to me. (N.B. He copied the
title of his story from the actual book).

Monday. 17th June.

I went to the fune
fare i went inon the big WLL
and i went on the bKtCar
and i went on the gst
tser and i wentOntle
Skateboard. ✓Excellent
work !

I went to the fun fair. I went on
the big wheel and I went on the
bumper car and I went on the ghost
train and I went on the skateboard.

Figure 14.3 *Paul's news about the funfair (June)*. Paul wrote this independently. He looked up the spelling of 'skateboard' in a class picture dictionary. Underneath, I have written down what he said when he read it back to me.

wanted to write. Their writing became strongly influenced by the stories they heard. They became more motivated to write not just stories but also their own everyday experiences which they began to see as being of value. Their talking and writing became, as Newland (1988) suggests, 'appraisals of their experiences'. Their positive attitudes to writing were enhanced when their work was redrafted and displayed around the classroom, giving their writing a purpose and an audience. The improvements in the children's writing were far greater than I had been expecting.

Conclusion

The power of story is immense. As has been highlighted by much current research, story has a significant place in the development of children's language and literacy skills as well as their psychological and emotional development. Through the use of story, the children in my investigation developed positive attitudes to reading and writing and their performances in both these areas improved. Their oral language also became more fluent. Through their exposure to story, the majority of them increased in self esteem and became happier and much more confident about their ability to read and write and take part in discussion. They began to find success in their reading which had not been the case while they were using the traditional reading scheme. Their growing enthusiasm for reading confirmed the views of both Waterland (1985) and Meek (1988) that in the traditional reading scheme 'very few become readers'. As Meek (1988) says, 'Literature makes readers in a way that reading schemes never can.'

Teachers need to be knowledgeable about the value of story and to use this often untapped resource in schools. They must keep up to date in the field of children's literature and surround their pupils with good quality books. Parents too need to be made aware of the importance of pre-school experience with stories and books.

The evidence in favour of the value of story is very weighty. If, as Betty Root, former director of the Reading Centre at Reading University, claims*, reading is no longer a 'normal' activity outside school and society in general does not see the importance of reading and story, then teachers in schools have a great responsibility to ensure that the next generation of adults do come to appreciate its significance.

* Betty Root, quoted by Amanda Mitchison in the *Independent Magazine*, 2/3/1991

Books referred to in this chapter

STORY CHEST READING BOOKS (Published by Arnold Wheaton, Exeter)

Cowley, J. & Melser. J (1980) *The Hungry Giant*
Cowley, J. & Melser. J (1988) *A Barrel of Gold*
Cowley, J. & Melser. J (1989) *The Sunflower that went Flop*
Eggleton, J. (1987) *The Old Oak Tree*

OTHER CHILDREN'S BOOKS

Ahlberg, A. & Ahlberg, J. (1989) *Burglar Bill*. London: Heinemann
Honeysett, M. (1984) *Animal Nonsense Rhymes*. London: Methuen
Kerr, J. (1968) *The Tiger Who Came to Tea*. London: Collins
Korky, P. (1987) *Winnie The Witch*. Oxford: University Press
McKee, D. (1980) *Not Now Bernard*. London: Arrow Books
Miles, B. (1987) *Teddy Takes a Train*. London: Grandreams
Southgate, V. (1980) *The Princess and the Frog*. Loughborough: Ladybird Books
Southgate, V. (1980) *The Magic Porridge Pot*. Loughborough: Ladybird
Thomson, P. (1986) *Can You Hear Me Grandad?* London: Gollancz
Tomlinson, J. (1973) *The Owl Who Was Afraid of the Dark*. Harmondsworth: Penguin

Chapter Fifteen

Finding Something to Read: How Libraries and School Bookshops Can Help Children to Become Readers

Sue Mansfield

Keen adult readers need no persuasion of the importance of libraries and bookshops in their lives. We all know the pleaure to be found in browsing and selecting from a huge range of books, and the sense of anticipation on arriving home with a stack of books under the arm. This love of books usually develops early in life. In this chapter I would like to suggest ways in which teachers, parents and librarians can work together through libraries and bookshops in schools to help to engender this enthusiasm for reading.

Public Libraries

Public libraries have long been involved in the promotion of children's literature. They have supported good writing and illustration for children through the annual Carnegie and Greenaway awards for the best story and best illustrated book for children, and as major purchasers of hardback books have been the mainstay of children's 'quality' publishing. Now, with more restricted budgets, greater emphasis is sometimes put on the purchase of fiction in paperback which, it is argued, is also a more attractive format to children, and this must inevitably have an effect on children's publishing. Indeed, some publishers have discontinued publication of hardbacks and bring new books out only in paperback form, and in shorter print runs, in order to keep costs down. Recent years have seen the development of collaborative publishing between publishers in different countries and a proliferation of series which are intended to develop a longterm adult market by creating a type of 'brand loyalty'.

All these factors have contributed to a boom in publishing for children and young people, of varying degrees of quality. The public library seeks to reflect this range of material and satisfy the demands of its clients whilst still promoting 'worthwhile' reading.

Public libraries have been a source of information and pleasure for both adults and children for many years. Children are frequently given a high priority and account for a substantial proportion of the books lent. Many public libraries have specialist children's librarians who are experts in children's literature and skilled at helping readers to find just the right book. Schools often take advantage of this by arranging regular class visits to their local library. Alternatively, the librarian may visit the school, either on a regular basis or for special occasions, for example to hold story sessions at book weeks or at school fairs.

Some librarians give a special emphasis to services to under-5's, arranging story sessions in the library, or visiting playgroups and nurseries as well as providing loans services to these groups. Comics and magazines may be provided, videos, story and music tapes and records lent, while some library services also stock computer games for older children. Many arrange extensive holiday-time activities, ranging from reading competitions to badge-making, facepainting and drama, for those of primary school age. All these attractions are designed to tempt children into the library, but its key functions remain the provision of information and the promotion of reading as an end and a joy in itself.

School Libraries

The school library can never replace the public library, with its large budget, specialised staff and network of support, but it can introduce children to the library 'atmosphere' so that they feel confident in approaching a public library. It also has a specific role in promoting the development of children's reading, both as an essential life-skill, as a vehicle for emotional and intellecual development, and above all for enjoyment.

As children develop as readers they need to have access to a wide range of reading material, which can either challenge and lead them on or reassure by familiarity. Many authors (Whitehead 1977, Southgate 1981, Ingham 1981, Thorpe 1988) have emphasised the enormous variety of titles read and enjoyed by the groups of children they studied. In some cases there were as many different 'favourite books' as the number of children in the sample group. This breadth of reading was found to depend upon there being a wide variety of material to choose from: the more choice there was, the more widely children read. This need for children to encounter a wide range of reading material has now been stressed in the National Curriculum programmes of study for English.

The school library can provide this diversity of reading, from 'classics' to comics, poetry and plays, stories and legends from many different cultures and books in the children's home languages or in dual language texts. Children will be encouraged to read by including in the library a wide variety of genres: many beginning readers prefer humorous books and adventure stories, while more confident readers may develop a taste for fantasy. Comics, magazines and children's newspapers attract children who may not feel confident with books. In the same way the library should offer books of varying levels of difficulty: committed readers may need to be extended by being encouraged to read more demanding texts, while less confident readers need the reassurance of plenty of books within their range.

There is a vast wealth of illustrated books to include in the library: many picture books such as those by Raymond Briggs or the *Where's Wally?* books by Martin Handford are seized upon by older children. Stories written by the children themselves will be enjoyed by others if included in the library. Audiotapes are now available of a wide variety of stories in many languages, in both abridged and complete form and these can be satisfying and enjoyable for both the confident and the more diffident reader. Some of the best of these are listed in the booklet *Hear to Read*. (This, and the other texts mentioned later, are included in the Resources List at the end of this chapter).

Non-fiction books may play an important part in stimulating a love of reading: many children who find difficulty in reading full length stories may tackle non-fiction books in which they are passionately interested. Some of the cartoon-style Usborne books or the Dorling Kindersley children's books with their very good quality illustrations and snatches of high-interest text can have this effect.

Books also need to look attractive and be in good condition: badly dilapidated books can be very offputting to the reader and undervalue their own content.

There has been much debate over where collections of books should be housed in the school and the relative merits of centralised and classroom libraries. The consensus of opinion seems to be that the best solution is a combination of the two, with books moving freely and frequently between them.

A class library has the advantage of having a limited range of books which can be deliberately targeted at that class. Children have the opportunity to browse through the books at odd times during the day and to return to old favourites. It is important, though, that a class library does not become tired and boring. Southgate (1981) found that there was a tendency for teachers to hold on to books which they had accumulated themselves over the years, even if these were damaged or unsuitable for the class they now taught. Books need to be regularly assessed for their appropriateness to the class in question and, apart from those favourites which the children return to time after time, moved termly between classes and the central library to keep the collections fresh.

Avid readers may soon exhaust the class library. Like adults, children need the opportunity to reject books which they think they will not enjoy. Indeed, selecting or rejecting are essential skills to be acquired by the developing reader (Cromer 1992). A central school library can encourage this ability by offering a greater variety of stories and non-fiction titles through which the child can browse at leisure than can the class library. It also allows less able readers the opportunity to look at books intended perhaps for a younger age group which she or he would disdain to be seen with in class. Unfortunately in some schools the library has to share a room with other activities: a library is most effective when it has a dedicated space, central in the school building and freely accessible to pupils at all times of day.

Studies have shown that most keen readers prefer to do their reading at home, preferably in bed. Most schools cannot provide that facility, but soft chairs or cushions and quiet spaces separated from the 'active' areas of the room by low-level bookcases create a cosy, inviting atmosphere. Books displayed face outwards attract the attention and invite browsing, a technique well exploited by successful commercial bookshops, but under-used in libraries.

Most libraries arrange fiction books in alphabetical order of the author's name. This is the most helpful arrangement for finding a specific book where the author is known. It can however be bewildering for children, who often have little idea of the names of authors they have enjoyed, and are confronted by an array of titles of varying difficulty and subject matter. How can they easily find the type of story they enjoy, at their own reading level? Schools take different approaches to solving this problem. Some colour code books according to their degree of difficulty. This enables a child to identify books which are appropriate to her/his own reading level, but may have the disadvantage of condemning the child to only reading at that level and from that particular collection of books. An alternative might be to shelve books in broad categories of difficulty, identified for example as 'Easy Reading' or 'Longer Reads'. This would allow children to choose from a wider range of material whilst still breaking the collection up into more accessible sections.

Similarly, a number of different approaches may be taken to identifying books of particular genres or styles. It is possible to buy spine labels from library suppliers which have symbols relating to different genres, such as a castle for fantasy or an animal for animal stories. Books may then be shelved in alphabetical order, with those books which fit into categories identified by these labels. Some schools adopt a policy often used in public libraries of shelving books of the same type together, for instance all funny stories, adventure stories etc. However, probably only about half of the library's stock will fit neatly into the chosen categories: the rest will still need to be shelved in alphabetical order. Another solution might be to make available to the children lists of books of different types, possibly with a brief outline of the story. Alternatively, a computer database could be set up, perhaps by the children themselves, which could produce lists of their favourite books by genre. Published versions of this type of database, such as *Fiction File,* may be adapted by schools to produce their own individualised version.

Whatever solution is adopted to arranging the books will not help library users unless it is made obvious to them. Attractive signs and labelling are essential for this.

Role of the Teacher/Librarian

Research into children's reading habits and accounts of successful school libraries emphasise the role of the teacher or librarian in bringing children and the right book together, through careful stock selection and the creation of an appropriate environment. Direct recommendation of books is not always successful: a survey published in 1992 by Enfield librarians found that recommendation by teacher or librarian was the method least used by children in selecting books. Adults can, however, encourage children to develop strategies for choosing books for themselves. Looking for authors or types of story that they have enjoyed before, thinking about what kinds of story they like, reading the 'blurb' on the cover of the book, looking at its length, size of print, illustrations etc. are all strategies which adults use a matter of course and which children can learn.

The teacher/librarian usually has the responsibility for selecting the stock for the school libarary while other staff may be buying books for their class collections. It therefore makes sense for the school to develop a coordinated policy for book purchase as part of an overall reading policy. This could establish criteria to be used in the selection of books and give guidance on diversity of text and illustration, on racism or sexism, and on the inclusion of 'sensitive' material, for example on sex education.

Wherever possible it is best to see books before purchasing them to ensure that they fit the school's needs. Many booksellers have extensive showrooms, whilst school book exhibitions provide an opportunity to see new and forthcoming publications. School Library Services, run by the local education authority or public library service, frequently offer schemes through which schools can purchase materials from a display collection put together by librarians. These are then supplied processed ready to be put straight on the school's library shelves.

Once the books are in school their presence needs to be advertised. Book related displays take time and effort but are very effective in raising awareness of books. They can be set up not only in the library but also in places around the school which children visit regularly, such as the hall or dining area. They need to be changed frequently to maintain interest, especially if the books can be borrowed and disappear quickly from the display. Displays can highlight new books in the library or focus on different themes, incorporating children's work and/or comments on books. Book reviews written by pupils, sometimes seen as a tedious exercise by the children themselves, take on meaning and give status to their author when bound together and displayed in the library for others to read.

Book clubs after school or at lunch time can give children valuable opportunities to discuss books with likeminded friends, to swap ideas and recommendations. Parents may enjoy helping and other interested adults, such as the local children's librarian, can be asked to attend to talk about new books. Reading aloud extracts from books can be an effective way of interesting children in stories which they might otherwise reject or overlook. Extracts can also be recorded on tape and left at a 'listening post' in the library or book corner for children to listen to at will. It will, of course, be necessary to have several copies of the recommended books so that children will not be disappointed by not being able to borrow them. Many ideas for interesting children in books and reading appear in the book *Reading Alive!*

Teachers do not always find time to keep up to date with children's books. The teacher/librarian can help colleagues by displaying new books and periodicals about children's books such as *Books for Keeps* or the *Times Educational Supplement* special bulletins in the staffroom. A 1992 *Daily Telegraph*/Gallup poll found that many parents have very little knowledge about modern, living children's authors. The school could help keep them informed by sending children home with attractive books to share with their families, by book displays or by the occasional item in the school newsletter, giving news of children's books, the school library or other reading activities. Some parents may be willing to help in the school library or book club.

Many schools now stage Book Weeks to promote reading and story to children, parents and, sometimes, the local community. These weeks often centre on visits by authors, illustrators or poets who read or hold workshops with the children. The visits are accompanied by displays and book-related activities held throughout the school, and usually by a sale of books. Whilst time-consuming for the organiser, Book Weeks are undoubtedly very successful in promoting the excitement of books. Further information on how to run a Book Week can be found in the Children's Book Foundation publication *The Book Week Handbook*. The CBF also organises an annual Children's Book Week to promote children's reading nationally and produces a Good Book Guide to the year's best books.

All these activities of course need time and support from colleagues within the school. Indeed, the DES in its 1989 publication *Better Libraries*, emphasised the need for all staff to be involved in the development of the library. Support outside the school can often be obtained from the local Schools Library Service. As well as the book purchase schemes mentioned earlier, these services usually loan collections of materials (not only books but audiovisual materials and, in some cases, artefacts) for different topics in the National Curriculum, and collections of fiction for leisure reading. Professional advice on setting up and running school libraries is often available and the librarians may also offer regular sessions on book selection when new publications and current trends in publishing may be discussed.

School Bookshops

The bookshop's role, though different, is complementary to that of the school library. The library provides the opportunity for children to experience a wide range of books of all styles and genres, but the books must always ultimately be given back. Owning their own books enables children to return time and time again to the tried and trusted favourites on their shelves. Ownership of books seems to imply ownership of reading itself; having one's own 'library' establishes the child as a reader in his/her own and other people's eyes. The school bookshop offers the opportunity of this ownership. It also enables the child to exercise her or his personal choice. When adults buy books for children they are heavily influenced by the books that they themselves read when young: top sellers of children's books in high street shops remain titles such as *Alice in Wonderland*, *Black Beauty* and *Treasure Island* (Horton 1992). In the comparative freedom of the school bookshop, children can make their own choices and take responsibility for their own reading. When the shop is run in a club-like atmosphere it additionally gives children the chance to discuss books between themselves, further developing their concept of themselves as readers.

A school bookshop might be seen as particularly useful in areas where there is no specialist commercial children's bookshop nearby. However, even when there is a good local shop a bookshop in school has a role, for it can stock a range of books particularly targeted at its child population and their families. It can also help parents and teachers to a greater awareness of contemporary children's books and demonstrate the school's commitment to children's literacy by bringing the books to the children.

The bookshop can take a variety of forms, from the termly book clubs such as the *Puffin Clubs* or *Letterbox Library*, through occasional books sales at school fairs or parents' evenings to a full-scale shop set up in its own area in the school and operating once a week or even more frequently.

Stock for these shops can be obtained either from national suppliers such as *Books for Students*, who also offer a good support service in the form of news sheets and promotional materials, or from local booksellers. These booksellers cannot usually offer the same support services, but the school bookshop organisers may benefit from the opportunity of choosing their own stock and developing a relationship with their often very knowledgeable local supplier.

The bookshop's wares are likely to be as varied as the children themselves and will reflect their interests and cultures. The main purpose of the shop is to promote reading as a leisure activity and it should put across the message that books are fun. Consequently its stock will have a slightly different emphasis to that of the school library which must cater for classroom research as well as children's individual interests, their 'serious' reading as well as entertainment. The shop might, for example, have a greater number of joke books than the library, or multiple copies of books currently enjoying a cult status, perhaps because they are tied to TV programmes or are being read to a class. Non-fiction books can be included to cater for individual children's enthusiasms, poetry to dip into and books from some of the many series such as the *Nancy Drew* books for the collectors among them. Children often like to buy books for their younger brothers and sisters, so it can be a good idea to include some board books for babies. Older children, especially ex-pupils, may visit the bookshop to look for books at the upper end of the age range. Price may be a factor in selecting books for the shop but above all, there should be plenty of choice and the stock should turn over frequently to ensure that it is always fresh.

Some schools open their shops at lunchtimes or after school, when parents can also visit; others give children access to the book shop or club during the school day. As with the library, the environment is very important: in a relaxed atmosphere children can make their purchases and discuss them with their friends. Teachers, parents or older children who run the shop should be helpful but not too intrusive: some children will want to choose for themselves, others may appreciate help with their choice if they are stuck. Adults can help by reading part or all of a book, discussing favourite authors or looking together at the synopsis on the cover of the book. In the end, though, the choice belongs to the children: they cannot be persuaded to buy or not buy books in the same way even that they can be prevailed upon to take out library books. However, it is possible to offer an exchange if a parent violently disagrees with their child's choice!

Books are fairly expensive commodities to children, so some bookclubs operate a savings scheme. Children can then bring in small amounts of money regularly and make their selections knowing that their chosen book will be reserved. This can be a powerful incentive: some children will save for many weeks for a highly prized book. The bookshop can also produce and sell its own book tokens: these can be promoted as useful birthday gifts.

As an extension of the school bookshop, a second-hand Swap Shop can be a useful way of circulating books within the school. A system can be operated, perhaps by older children, whereby books brought in to swap are allocated a number of tokens according to their condition, length and general desirability. These tokens can then be exchanged for others from the Swap Shop. It may be possible to use the Swap Shop to offer the chance of book ownership to children who are not able or willing to use the new book shop.

Like the library, the bookshop will need regular promoting to keep interest alive throughout the school. Posters can remind children and parents of its time and place, bookshop news can appear in school newsletters and circulars and book-related competitions can be held with book tokens as prizes. The best incentive to selling books, though, is the visit of an author or illustrator; then the bookshop must be ready with multiple copies of their books.

In Conclusion

Children developing as readers need choice and there is now a vast and sometimes bewildering range of published books from which they can choose. The library and school bookshop together can offer children this choice in a congenial environment, helping them to find the books that will stimulate or entertain them and develop the skills which will allow their reading to progress. These are the places where they can come to see and value themselves and each other as readers and form a habit which will give pleasure for life.

Resource List

Books for Keeps
Magazine of the School Bookshop Association. Useful reviewing journal.
Also publishes articles about books and authors. 6 issues per year.
£11.40 (UK)
Books for Keeps, 6 Brightfield Road, Lee, London SE12 8QF. (081 852
4953)

School Librarian
Journal of the School Library Association (SLA). The SLA is a useful
source of information about school libraries, producing a number of
publications. £20 annual subscription includes journal. 4 issues per
year.
School Librarian, The School Library Association, Liden Library, Barrington
Close, Liden, Swindon SN3 6HP (0793 617838)

Children's Book Foundation
Storehouse of information about children's books and authors, with display
collection of all children's books published in the last two years. Publi-
cations include annual *Good Book Guide* and *Book Fax*, a wide-ranging
directory of current information on children's books and reading.
Redford, Rachel (1986) *Hear to read*. London: National Book League.
Annotated list of audiotapes. Dated but still useful as a guide.
Gawith, Gwen (1990) *Reading Alive*. London: Black. Full of practical
ideas for promoting reading.
Fiction File: Lower and Middle Anglia Television, 1991
Datafile of fiction for ages 5–13 originated by Bedfordshire Youth Librari-
ans and Schools Library Service.

Books for Students
Complete school bookshop service.
Books for Students, Bird Road, Heathcote, Warwick CV34 6TB. (0926
813910)

Letterbox Library
Children's book club offering non-sexist and multi-cultural books for
children.
Letterbox Library, 8 Bradbury St., London N16 8JN. (071 254 1640)

Puffin Book Clubs
For three age groups, run only through schools and playgroups.
Puffin Book Clubs, 7 Wrights Lane, London W8 5TZ. (071 938 2200)

How to set up and run a school bookshop School Bookshop Association,
1991. Very valuable booklet on the hows and whys of setting up a
school bookshop. Now unfortunately out of print.

Bibliography

Adams, R. (1974) 'Watership Authorship', *Bradfield College Chronicle*, Autumn, pp.5–10

Applebee, A. (1978) *The Child's Concept of Story*. Chicago: University Press

Appleyard, J.A. (1990) *Becoming a Reader: the Experience of Fiction from Childhood to Adulthood*. Cambridge: University Press

Ari, M. & Gonen (1989) 'Picture Story Books and Language Development: a Turkish Study', in *Bookbird*, No. 27 (3)

Barrs, M. (1988) 'Maps of Play', in (eds.) Meek, M. & Mills, C. *Language and Literacy in the Primary School*. Lewes: Falmer Press

Barrs, M. et al. (1988) *The Primary Language Record Handbook*. London: CLPE

Barrs, M. (1990) 'Children's Theories of Narrative', *English in Education*, Vol. 24, No. 1, Spring 1990

Bettelheim, B. (1976/8) *The Uses of Enchantment*. Harmondsworth: Penguin

Brown, J.R. (1976) *Children and Television*. London: Macmillan

Buckingham, D. (1992) 'Why Television Literacy?' in Dombey, H. & Robinson, M. (eds.) *Literacy for the Twentyfirst Century*. Falmer: Brighton Polytechnic

Bruner, J. (1986) *Actual Minds Possible Worlds*. Cambridge Mass.: Harvard University Press.

Butler, D. (1979) *Cushla and her Books*. London: Hodder & Stoughton

Chambers, A. (1984) *Introducing Books to Children*. (2nd edition) London: Heinemann

Chambers, A. (1985) *Booktalk*. London: Bodley Head

Chapman, L.J. (1983) *Reading Development and Cohesion*. London: Heinemann

Chapman, L.J. (1987) *Reading From 5–11 Years*. Milton Keynes: Open

University

Chieruzzi, A. (1986) *An Analysis of and a Comparison Between Attitudes to Reading as Displayed by Two Groups of Eight Year Old Children Taught by Contrasting Methods.* University of Surrey (Roehampton Institute): Unpublished MA Dissertation

Clare, J. 'Hands Up: Who's Read This? *Daily Telegraph*: Children's Book Week Special, 2nd October 1992

Clay, M.M. (1991) *Becoming Literate.* Auckland: Heinemann

Corcoran, B. & Evans, E. (eds.) (1987) *Readers, Texts, Teachers* Milton Keynes: Open University

Cook, E. (1976) *The Ordinary and the Fabulous.* Cambridge: University Press

Cox, B. (1989) *English for Ages Five to Sixteen.* London: D.E.S.

Crago, H. & M. (1983) *Prelude to Literacy.* Illinois: University Press

Cromer, C. (1992) *An Investigation of how Children make Independent Book Choices.* University of Surrey (Roehampton Institute): Unpublished BA dissertation

Cullingford, C. (1979) 'Why Children Like Enid Blyton', in *New Society* 9/8/79

Cullingford, C. (1984) *Children and Television.* Aldershot: Gower

Davies, F. (1986) *Books in the School Curriculum: A Compilation and Review of Research Relating to Voluntary and Intensive Reading.* London: Educational Publishers Council & National Book League

Department of Education and Science (1975) *A Language for Life* (The Bullock Report). London: H.M.S.O.

Dias, P, & Hayhoe, M. (1988) *Developing Response to Poetry.* Milton Keynes: Open University

Dickinson, P. 'A Defence of Rubbish', in Fox. G. et al. (eds.) (1976) *Writers, Critics and Children.* London: Heinemann

Dixon, B. (1978) *Catching Them Young.* London: Pluto

Doonan, J. (1983) 'Talking Pictures: A New Look at *Hansel and Gretel*, in *Signal* no. 42, Sept. 1983

Doonan, J. (1993) *Looking at Pictures in Picture Books.* Stroud: Thimble Press

Durkin, K. (1985) *Television, Sex Roles and Children: A Developmental Social Psychological Account.* Milton Keynes: Open University

Francis, M. (1989) 'In my Opinion . . .: Central or Classroom Collections', in *School Librarian* Vol. 37. No. 1, Feb. 1989.

Fry, D. (1985) *Children Talk about Books: Seeing themselves as Readers.* Milton Keynes: Open Uinversity

Goodwin, P. (1992) Unpublished MA Coursework, University of Surrey (Roehampton Institute)

Gorman, T. (1987) *Pupils' Attitudes to Reading*. Walton Thames: NFER/Nelson

Graham, J. (1990) *Pictures on the Page*. Sheffield: NATE

Greenfield, G. (1992) 'Enid Blyton Remembered', *The Bookseller* (21 August)

Griffith, P. (1987) *Literary Theory and English Teaching*. Milton Keynes: Open University

Grugeon, E. & Walden, P. (1978) *Literature and Learning*. London: Ward Lock

Halliday, M.A.K. & Hasan, R. (1976) *Cohesion in English*. London: Longman

Handford, M. (1987) *Where's Wally?* London: Walker Books

Hardy, B. (1968) 'Towards a poetics of fiction: Approach through Narrative', in (ed.) Meek, M. et al. (1977) *The Cool Web*. London: Bodley Head

Hayhoe, M. & Parker, S. (1990) (eds.) *Reading and Response*. Milton Keynes: Open University

Hearn, B. (1992) *A Linguistic Comparison of the Texts Used by Two Reception Classes*. University of Surrey (Roehampton Institute): Unpublished MA dissertation

Heath, S.B. (1983) *Ways with Words*. Cambridge: University Press

Heeks, P. (1981) *Choosing and Using Books in the First School*. London: Macmillan

Hibbs, E. et al. (1992) 'The Case for Categorisation: an Investigation of Children's Selection Methods', in *Youth Library Review*, No. 14

Himmelweit, H.T., Oppenheim, A.N. & Vince, P. (1958) *Television and the Child*. Oxford: University Press

H.M.I. (1989) *Better Libraries: Good Practice in Schools*. London: D.E.S.

H.M.I. (1990) *Library Provision and Use in 42 Primary Schools*. London: DES

Horton, B. (1992) *Adults, Children and Books*. University of Surrey (Roehampton Institute): Unpublished BA dissertation

Howe, A. & Johnson, J. (1992) *Common Bonds; Storytelling in the Classroom*. London: Hodder & Stoughton

Ingham, J. (1981) *Books and Reading Development: the Bradford Book Flood*. London: Heinemann

Ingham, J. (1982) 'Middle School Children's Responses to Enid Blyton: the Bradford Book Flood Experiment', *Journal of Research in Reading*, vol. 5, no. 1

Iser, W. (1974) *The Implied Reader*. Baltimore: Johns Hopkins University Press

Iser, W. (1978) *The Act of Reading*. Baltimore: Johns Hopkins University

Press

Kerr, P. (1982) 'Classic Serials – To Be Continued', *Screen* vol. 23, no. 1

Kingman, J. (1988) *Report of the Committee of Inquiry into the Teaching of the English Language*. London: H.M.S.O.

Kingman, L. (1965) (ed.) *Newberry and Caldecott Medal Books: 1956–1965*. Boston, Mass.: The Horn Book

Kinnnell, M. (1992) 'Managing School Library Services post ERA *Youth Library Review* No.13, Spring. 1992

Knott, R. (1985) *The England Department in a Changing World*. Milton Keynes: Open University

Knundsen Linauer, S.L. (1988) 'Wordless Books: An Approach to Visual Literacy', in *Children's Literature in Education*, Autumn 1988, vol. 19 (3)

Landes, S. (1985) 'Picture Books as Literature', in *Children's Literature Association Quarterly*, vol. 10, no. 2

Lathey, G. (1988) 'Taking on the Transformers', in Mills, C. & Timson, L (eds.) (1988) *Looking at Language in the Primary School*. London: NATE

Lutrario, C. (ed.) (1990) *Hooked on Books: Children Reading Fiction*. London: Harcourt Brace Jovanovitch

Marshall, M. (1988) *An Introduction to the World of Children's Books*. Aldershot: Gower

Meek, M. et al. (eds.) (1977) *The Cool Web: the Pattern of Children's Reading*. London: Bodley Head

Meek, M. (1982) 'The Role of the Story', in *Story in the Child's Changing World*, Proceedings of International Board on Books for Young People, Churchill College Cambridge, 1982

Meek, M. (1988) *How Texts Teach what Readers Learn*. Stroud: Thimble Press

Meek, M. (1991) *On Being Literate*. London: Bodley Head

Meek, M. (1992) 'Known Voices in a New Key' in Kimberley, K. et al. (eds.) (1992) *New Readings*. London: A. & C.Black

Melody, W, (1973) *Children's Television: the Economics of Exploitation*. London: Yale University Press

Miller, B.M. & Field, E.W. (1957) *Caldecott Medal Books: 1938–1957*. Boston, Mass.: The Horn Book

Moss, E. (1990) 'A Certain Particularity: an Interview with Janet and Alan Ahlberg', in *Signal* 61, Jan. 1990

Newland, A. (1988) 'This is your Life', *Language Matters* Nos. 2 & 3, pp.1–4 London: C.L.P.E.

Pain-Lewins, H. (1990) 'Reading for Pleasure and the School Library', *Reading* Vol. 24, No. 3

Pain-Lewins, H. & Kinnell, M. (1989) *Book Acquisition and Use by Young People: A Review of Recent Research Initiatives.* London: British National Bibliography Research Fund

Paley, V.G. (1981) *Wally's Stories.* Cambridge, Mass.: Harvard University Press

Paley, V.G. (1984) *Boys and Girls Superheroes in the Doll Corner* Chicago: University Press

Protherough, R. (1983) *Developing Response to Fiction.* Milton Keynes: Open University

Reynolds, K. (1991) 'Books on the Box: the BBC Chronicles of Narnia', *Critical Survey*, vol 3, no. 3

Rose, J. (1984) *The Case of Peter Pan: the Impossibility of Children's Fiction.* London: Macmillan

Rosen, H. (1988) 'Stories of Stories', in (ed.) Rosen, B. (1988) *And None of It was Nonsense.* London: Mary Glasgow Publications

Rustin, M. & M. (1987) *Narratives of Love and Loss: Studies in Modern Children's Fiction.* New York: Verso

Sarland, C. (1991) *Young People Reading: Culture and Response.* Milton Keynes: Open University

Sarland, C. (1983) 'Combination', in *Signal* September 1983

Sharp, L. (1988) 'Library Books and Reluctant Readers', *Reading* Vol. 22, No. 3

Shavit, Z. (1986) *Poetics of Children's Literature.* Georgia: University Press

Smith, F. (1982) *Reading.* Cambridge: University Press

Smith, F. (1988) *Joining the Literacy Club.* London: Heinemann

Smith, M. & Hoffman, M. (1992) 'How Safe is Your School's Library?' *Books for Keeps* No. 72

Southgate, V. et al. (1981) *Extending Beginning Reading.* London: Heinemann

Stibbs, A. (1978) *Assessing Children's Language.* London: Ward Lock Educn. and NATE

Stibbs, A. (1991) *Reading Narrative as Literature: Signs of Life.* Milton Keynes: Open University

Styles, M., Bearne, E., & Watson, V. (eds.) (1992) *After Alice: Exploring Children's Literature.* London: Cassell

Thorpe, D. (1988) *Reading for Fun: A Study of How Parents and Libraries encouraged Children 9–12 to read for enjoyment.* Cranfield: Cranfield Press

Thwaite, A. (1990) *A.A. Milne.* London: Faber

Tolkein, J.R.R. (1964) 'Children and Fairy Stories', In (ed.) Egoff, S. et al. (1980) *Only Connect: Readings on Children's Literature.* Toronto:

Oxford University Press

Townsend, J.R. (1990) *Written for Children*. London: Bodley Head

Trelease, J. (1984) *The Read-Aloud Handbook*. Harmondsworth: Penguin

Tucker, N. (1971) 'Learning to Read Pictures', in *Times Literary Supplement* 2nd July, 1971

Tucker, N. (1975) 'The Blyton Enigma', in *Children's Literature in Education*, No. 19

Tucker, N. (1981) *The Child and the Book: A Psychological and Literary Exploration*. Cambridge: University Press

Tudge, C. (1989) 'If we could talk to the animals', *New Scientist*, 4/2/89

Vygotsky, L.S. (1978) *Mind in Society*. Cambridge, Mass.: Harvard University Press

Wade, B. (1984) *Story at Home and School* (Educational Review Occasional Paper No. 10). Edgebaston: University of Birmingham

Wall, B. (1991) *The Narrator's Voice*. London: Macmillan

Walsh, M. (1991) *Story and the Development of Children's Literacy*. University of Surrey (Roehampton Institute): Unpublished B Ed dissertation

Walsh, S. (1992) *Whispering Wishes in the Park*. University of Surrey (Roehampton Institute): Unpublished MA dissertation

Waterland, L. (1985) *Read with me*. Stroud: Thimble Press

Wells, G. (1986) *The Meaning Makers*. London: Heinemann

Wells, G. (1982) *Language, Learning and Education*. Bristol: University Department of Education

West, A. (1986) 'The Production of Readers' *English Magazine* 17, pp.4–9, London: ILEA.

White, D. (1954) *Books Before Five*. Oxford: University Press

Whitehead. F. et al. (1977) *Children and their Books*. London: Macmillan

Winick, M.P. & Winick, C. (1979) *The Television Experience: What Children See*. London: Sage Publications

Wright, A. (1984) 'Illustrations, Infants and Language Development', in *English in Education*, vol. 18, no. 3, Autumn 1984

Index

Notes on Contributors

FIONA COLLINS
is a senior lecturer in English at Roehampton

SUSAN FREMANTLE
is a lecturer in English in Education at Roehampton

MARTIN GODLEMAN
is head of English in a boys' secondary school in Surrey

BARBARA HEARN
is head of a primary school in London

PHILIPPA HUNT
is a lecturer in English in Education at Roehampton

NICOLA HUMBLE
is a lecturer in English at Roehampton

ALISON KELLY
is a lecturer in English in Education at Roehampton

SUE MANSFIELD
is an Education Librarian with responsibility for the School Experience collection at Roehampton

JACQUIE NUNN
is a lecturer in English in Education at Roehampton

PAT PINSENT
is a principal lecturer in English at Roehampton

KIM REYNOLDS
is a lecturer in English at Roehampton

CATHERINE SHELDON
teaches in a secondary school on Merseyside

MARY WALSH
is a primary school teacher in London

SHARON WALSH
is head of a primary school in London